"Mr. Jefferson remarked that 'it is the manners and spirit of a people which preserve a republic in vigor. A degeneracy in these is a canker which soon eats to the heart of its laws and constitution.'"

— Albert Jay Nock, *A Study In Manners*

PLAGIARISM AND THE CULTURE WAR

PLAGIARISM AND THE CULTURE WAR

The Writings of Martin Luther King, Jr., and Other Prominent Americans

THEODORE PAPPAS

HALLBERG PUBLISHING CORPORATION

Nonfiction Book Publishers – ISBN 0-87319

Tampa, Florida 33623

Publisher's Cataloging-in-Publication

Pappas, Theodore.
  Plagiarism and the Culture War : The Writings of Martin Luther King, Jr., and Other
  Prominent Americans / Theodore Pappas. — Rev. and Expanded Ed.
  p. cm.
  Includes bibliographical references and index.
  "Abbreviated 1st ed. published as The Martin Luther King, Jr., Plagiarism Story, by
  the Rockford Institute of Rockford, Ill., in 1994."
  1. Plagiarism — United States. 2. King, Martin Luther, Jr., 1929-1968 — Ethics.
  3. Culture conflict — United States. 4. Literary ethics — Social aspects — United
  States. I. Title.
PN168.K56P37 1998   818'.54
                                 QBI98-365

HALLBERG PUBLISHING CORPORATION
P.O. Box 23985 • Tampa, Florida 33623
Phone 1-800-633-7627 • Int'l. 1-941-322-2514
Fax 1-800-253-READ • Fax Int'l. 1-941-322-1331

In Memory of My Mother
Jean Hood Pappas

"No more evidence is needed; the verdict is in: nothing is more intolerant of a diversity of opinion than a 'liberal' society touting the virtues of tolerance and diversity."

CONTENTS

1   Foreword: *Eugene Genovese*

9   Foreword To First Edition: *Jacob Neusner*

19   Introduction

21   Chapter 1 – Plagiarism and the Culture War

65   Chapter 2 – The Strange Career of Martin Luther King, Jr.'s Dissertation

85   Chapter 3 – The Anatomy of a Scoop

105   Chapter 4 – Plagiarism for Progress

123   Chapter 5 – Houdinis of Time

137   Chapter 6 – Truth or Consequences

149   Chapter 7 – Scholarship and the King Legacy

173   Chapter 8 – Death Threats, Lies, and the Future of American Culture

189   Notes and References

201   Index

FOREWORD

Theodore Pappas is a foolish man. Against all evidence, he believes that integrity and professional ethics should count for something among the academics who orate on them at every college commencement. To make matters worse, he considers plagiarism a serious matter and thinks he can try our patience with a recitation of its destructive course in intellectual life. No wonder, then, that he could not find a commercial or university press to publish the first edition of this book that reviews the general problem of fraud and plagiarism today and highlights as a case study how the academy and the media covered up and whitewashed the scandal of Martin Luther King, Jr.'s plagiarisms. And no wonder that the first edition of this book, published by The Rockford Institute as *The Martin Luther King, Jr., Plagiarism Story* in 1994, got the silent treatment from the media and from scholarly journals.

As Jacob Neusner explained in his splendid foreword to the first edition, reprinted in this volume, "The following book records, among other things, how the academic world and our opinion-makers in the media have confronted the fact that a revered American was a plagiarist." Pappas has proceeded responsibly and deserves to be heard and to have his arguments answered. But he has not been answered because the essentials of his indictment are unanswerable. Particularly interesting are the commu-

1

nications, quoted and reprinted in this volume, from administrators at Boston University, where King did his graduate work in theology and philosophy. Their sole content consists of evasions, of attempts to discredit King's critics. They do not refute any of the principal points in Pappas's indictment.

As is clear in the first two volumes of *The Papers of Martin Luther King, Jr.*, edited by Clayborne Carson, King plagiarized throughout his career as an undergraduate and graduate student. Those volumes contain carefully honed footnotes that expose King's wholesale lifting of passages, large and small, on a scale so vast as to leave no room for excuse or exculpation. Pappas includes a few, which are damaging enough to make his case, but, by far, the greater damage has been done by the editors of King's papers in a remarkably painstaking job of detective work. The extensive plagiarism in King's doctoral dissertation carried forward a long-standing practice. Yet, instead of getting sober appraisals of the record and reflections on its significance for King's legacy and for the academic world that permitted such violations of professional ethics, we have been inundated with silence — silence punctuated by occasional excuses.

Pappas has every right to argue that King's academic career will not stand scrutiny. It might be said in King's defense that his professors share the blame. But that shared blame would not constitute much of a defense under any circumstances, and it becomes feeble in the light of King's oft-expressed insistence on individual responsibility. King's teachers, as Pappas shows, let him flout scholarly procedures they had ostensibly trained him to observe.

Some critics have suggested that Boston University treated black students with racist contempt, expecting much less from them than they expected from white students. Outraged professors and administrators at

Boston University have gone to great lengths to assure the world that the charge is a damnable lie and that King's teachers never dreamed of making such a distinction. I am prepared to believe them. Reviewing the performance of King's teachers at Boston Divinity School, as chronicled in the second volume of King's papers, I find altogether plausible the thought that they were training white students as miserably as they were training black, and that they themselves were inadequately prepared in the subjects in which they claimed expertise. Personally, I would rather be convicted of racism than of professional incompetence, but that, after all, is a matter of taste.

The evidence for King's shortcomings runs deeper than even Pappas or harsher critics have yet discerned. King's graduate school papers, as well as the dissertation, were full of errors that competent professors would have subjected to stern criticism. Instead, his principal professors, Edgar Sheffield Brightman and L. Harold DeWolf, both of whom enjoyed reputations as theological scholars, gave King A's without a hint that they spotted the errors. The papers they praised highly made a mess out of Calvinist and Barthian theology. King's papers demonstrated a misreading of Calvin's view of predestination, an ignorance of the work of leading Calvinist theologians, and disregard of Karl Barth's most important work. King faked a reading knowledge of German. He could not read the early work of Paul Tillich, one of the two subjects of his doctoral dissertation; instead, he pretended to have done so by the device of occasional quotations he lifted from secondary works. Even before writing the dissertation, King's lack of German led him into a critique of Barth that centered on interpretations Barth had long before revised in *Church Dogmatics*, his 14-volume magnum opus, the first six volumes of which were then, except for a portion of volume one, available only in German.

King's teachers made no attempt to point out that his critique was obsolete, although they were themselves reading Barth. DeWolf published several lengthy attacks on Barth (in which he demonstrated his own incompetence). And DeWolf had no excuse for not knowing of Hans Urs von Balthasar's powerful *The Theology of Karl Barth*, then available in German, which would have spared him and King embarrassment on the very point of dialectical method on which King focused.

As for the doctoral dissertation, King wrote it while he was serving as a full-time pastor, subject to round-the-clock demands on his time. Understandably but not excusably, he cut every possible corner. Well, it may not be excusable to many of us, but it is excusable to Professor S. Paul Schilling, the second reader of King's thesis at Boston University, who has offered it as a defense. King had one claim to making a contribution to scholarship in his dissertation, "A Comparison of the Conceptions of God in the Thinking of Paul Tillich and Henry Nelson Wieman," and in it he does provide a useful comparative analysis of the theology of Wieman and Tillich. King plagiarized much of the specifics, but his comparison was itself thoughtful and worth reading. Hence Schilling had some justification for standing by the summary judgment in his second-reader's report: "The comparisons and evaluations are fair-minded, balanced, and cogent. The author shows sound comprehension and critical capacity." All of which is true enough so far as it goes. But Boston University's report on King's plagiarism does not mention that the dissertation was approved despite King's failure to make the important if limited corrections Schilling had called for.

That Schilling, who was then a vulnerable assistant professor, kept silent may be excused as an act of self-preservation. In view of the wonderful practices common throughout academia, opening his mouth might easily have finished his career, and I am not among those who invoke principle to demand that others immolate themselves. But Schilling maintains his silence on this point even now. And that goes down hard.

On one important matter I must dissent from Pappas's indictment. He assails Clayborne Carson, the editor of the King Papers, for trying to cover up the plagiarism. As evidence, he cites numerous dissembling remarks that Carson made to the press when he began to be besieged with the swelling rumors about plagiarism and about the delay in bringing out the volumes of King's papers — a delay readily explained by editorial and other unrelated difficulties. The volumes of King's papers are meticulously edited, replete with footnotes that expose the plagiarism in excruciating detail. Pappas disagrees with the editors' interpretations of the plagiarism, and those interpretations may be hotly contested, but they do not affect the main point — the responsibility of the editors *qua* editors to lay out the evidence clearly and fully in the volumes they were editing. And that is precisely what they did.

As for Carson's early dissembling, I only hope that he is a Catholic, not a Protestant. For he committed a venial, not a mortal, sin and should be willing to take his chances on a short stint in purgatory. Speculation about his early denials are probably uncalled for, but I shall speculate anyway. Putting myself in his place, I would have wanted time to figure out how to break the news without stoking the appetite of racists; to prepare the King family as gently as possible and to enlist their support for a policy of full disclosure; and to wait until the research into the plagiarism had gone far enough to permit a careful judgment on just how extensive and deep it was.

Be that as it may, Theodore Pappas responsibly reviews King's plagiarism and the dishonorable behavior of academia and the media in this case and many others, and this brave book deserves a wide reading. You could argue that, given the proliferation of journals and alternative presses, everything eventually finds its way into print, but, even were this the case, important books get ignored wholesale or in part. In decades past, it was books that disturbed liberal complacency that were abused or made to disappear; in these days of the Culture War, it is books that rankle the complacency of the multicultural left. The commitment to integrity, professional ethics, fearless scholarship, and freedom of thought only goes so far.

Eugene Genovese
Distinguished Scholar in Residence,
University Center in Georgia

FOREWORD TO FIRST EDITION

This book records, among other things, how the academic world and our opinion-makers in the media have confronted the fact that a revered American was a plagiarist. The Reverend Martin Luther King, Jr.'s place in history is secure by reason of his memorable leadership of the civil rights movement. But those who have transformed him into an icon to be polished, instead of accepting him as a great man whose great deeds are to be emulated but whose considerable flaws are to be noted and avoided, want more. They define the politically correct judgment of King's life in terms that defy plausibility, that deny the man that humanity which rendered all the more sublime the achievements of his mature intellect: his public advocacy of nonviolence; his insistence — sorely missed today — that a single law govern white and black, Jew and Gentile, man and woman; and, above all, his courageous leadership of black Americans in a time of crisis.

When Theodore Pappas began discussing King's plagiarisms in 1990, the engines of political correctness raised steam and sounded their whistles. The mere fact that this book could find no publisher other than Mr. Pappas's own sponsor makes one wonder what need we have for guarantees of freedom of the press — let alone free speech. The press, after all, rarely accords a cordial welcome to those who violate its rigid norms of what may and may not be thought, therefore said. But if the press and world of publishing may find little in which to take pride in their response to the embarrassing facts turned up in his book, what is to be said of the academy?

The answer elucidated in this book did not offer much reassurance to those who hope that this country's universities may meet their responsibility to truth, integrity, and national renewal. The press and the publishing world, which exist to make money, have fared no better: publishers want to sell more than one book, and publishing this one — so they feared — would mark them for a long, dismal future. But the press and the book publishers claim no moral authority; everyone knows who they are and what they do. By contrast, the professors, provosts, deans, and presidents addressed in this book all represent themselves as scholars; they have taken learning as their vocation and so profess to care for what is true and can be shown to be true; and, we must not forget, all of them also enjoy lifetime tenure in their academic positions, if not in their administrative ones.

So society accords them security and privilege, hoping in exchange to gain the benefit of objective criticism and sustained truth-telling. Then, while elements of the press can always be found to form the exception to the rule of cowardice, on the one side, and rigid conformity, on the other, what excuse can we find to explain the conduct, in the present controversy, of those who, impregnable in tenure, endowed with the prestige accruing to the academy, protected from reprisal by law and custom, turned their back on the facts? Or, worse still, what are we to make of those who explain away and justify in terms of the peculiar culture of black Americans actions that, when done by other Americans, are penalized? Demeaning to blacks and a self-serving cover for deep racism, the excuses for King's thefts — that is, his using without attribution enormous tracts of writing not his own — bear a brutal judgment. Only the academy as we know it in these troubled times can issue racist judgments in the name of intellect, inventing for the occasion categories and classifications to stigmatize entire races as subject to a moral law different from that ordinary folk obey.

And that meretricious, condescending defense of King's thievery is precisely what people offered when Pappas asked his tough, embarrassing questions. They lied, they told half-truths, they made up fables, they did everything they could but address facts; three enlightened individuals even threatened his life. In the face of their own university's rules against plagiarism, Boston University's academic authorities and professors somehow found excuses for King's plagiarism. They found extenuating circumstances, they reworded matters to make them sound less dreadful, they compromised their own university's integrity and the rules supposedly enforced to defend and protect the processes of learning and the consequent degrees. They called into question the very standing of the university as a place where cheating is penalized and misrepresentation condemned. And all this, why? I suspect it stems from insufficient faith in the authentic achievements of Martin Luther King, Jr., from a greater concern to explain away the flaws of his life's record than to set them in the balance against the glories of his brief, courageous life.

Why, we therefore have to ask ourselves, must Martin Luther King, Jr., be remembered in an implausible image of perfection, when the full and human man leaves a so much greater heritage of human achievement: courage, perseverance, insistence upon the equality of every American before the law, uncompromising demand for justice for each of us? That did not suffice, and instead a systematic campaign to discredit irrefutable facts aimed at giving the country a Martin Luther King, Jr., whom everyone must confront not as a great man but only as a perfect God. But (in the language of Christianity, which King spoke) only One was God Incarnate, and only One has risen from the dead. Was not King all the greater for the natural man he transcended in his quest for justice for all Americans? Is not the civil rights movement of the 1960's, which did tear down the old American structure of legal racism, a monument to King's capacity for moral leadership of all Americans? Did this man not die — knowingly give up his life in a dangerous venture — for the things he espoused?

Yes, King was all the greater, the movement does serve as his monument, and the man knew precisely the risks he took and the price he would pay. What more can a man achieve with scarcely four decades on this earth than King achieved for blacks among all Americans? What more do his latter-day apologists want for him? What Pappas brings into question is not King's greatness, but the divinity that has descended about him and isolated and alienated him from the realm of the human, which he in his life graced more than disgraced — much more.

Pappas's observations about Samuel Taylor Coleridge and King — "both men plagiarized some of their most influential prose and were publicly exposed as pilferers only after death" — brought to mind the critical question for the academy. What was at stake in trying to suppress what in the end would inexorably rise to the surface? Rumor has it that King's doctoral committee recognized the problem of plagiarism and instructed him to provide the documentation that the academy's ethics required. The dissertation was filed and accepted without the corrections and revisions being made; no one followed up. That rumor evidently means to mitigate the stark and awful truth that Boston University bestowed an earned doctorate for work that did not meet the accepted standards of honesty and scholarship.

If the story is so, then King presumably deposited whatever was in hand; no one checked. But in universities, we are supposed to check; that is what we are paid to do. Society assigns us the task of intellectual integrity: someone out there has to say how things are, without bias or cunning. That is why King was not well-served; the faculty owed him their careful criticism not only of his ideas and mode of setting them forth, demonstrating them, addressing possible objections to them, but also of his presentation of those ideas in written form, including the usual references to what he had consulted — all the more, what he had quoted. The awful suspicion lurks that a lower standard applied to blacks than whites, and it is difficult to suppress the question of whether the professors at Boston University might have imputed to their black students lesser capacities than those they saw in whites.

In the past few years Pappas has found little grounds for confidence in the academy's integrity. Corrupted by its own peculiar brand of tolerance, the academy tergiversated. Ignoble synonyms may also serve: apostatize, desert, rat, renounce, repudiate, dodge, evade, hedge, pussyfoot, shuffle, sidestep, and weasel. The letter from Jon Westling of Boston University, reprinted in Chapter Two, which denied that anyone had "ever found any nonattributed or misattributed quotations, misleading paraphrases, or thoughts borrowed without due scholarly reference in any of [the dissertation's] 343 pages," did set the record straight — but as Pappas shows, it was straight to hell, not exactly the direction the acting president of Boston University had in mind. What Westling revealed was his university's policy, which was concede nothing, especially not the facts. That makes all the more stark the side-by-side citations of King's and Jack Boozer's writings. The comparison opens the question of whether, without Boozer, King had a dissertation at all. One need not follow Pappas's righteous — and understandable — indignation to its end, of stripping King of his degree and replacing it with an honorary doctorate. Posthumous acts of this kind strike me as vengeful, but also vacuous, no less than posthumous honors, for that matter. But, in the context of a breaking story, addressing people who in defending an icon undertook to fabricate a massive tissue of lies, who can fail to grasp the provocation?

Charles Babington's article "Embargoed" from the January 28, 1991, issue of the *New Republic*, reprinted in this volume, revealed the many publishers and editors who suppressed the facts. But he does not list the writers and scholars — "several historians" — who declined to write the story. Martin Peretz of the *New Republic* explained that the story had "racial overtones." But acts of omission mattered more. It is what people did not say, would not do, declined to publish, refused to investigate, that shows us the true character of thought-control today. Political correctness ("racial overtones" indeed!), with its selective agenda of bigotry to be condemned as against that to be tolerated or dismissed, with its power to explain away what elsewhere it finds intolerable — that political correctness is exposed in these pages.

Its affect upon the academy, its corruption of the very character of academic research in history and other humanities, as well as in the social sciences — none can now foresee the long-term effects of political correctness. But those of us who remember what 12 years of Nazism did to the German universities — the death of intellect, the end of integrity — cannot look with much confidence into the future of those many, formerly elite American universities that are complicit in the sad story told in these pages. Nazism left German universities empty of all intellectual vitality. With investigating committees proliferating and free speech now subject to violent challenge on our campuses, who can tell me how our universities differ from those of Nazi Germany, except in the detail that there the right defined the norm and here the left does? There the Jews were evicted, here those not among the scheduled castes — those not black, not female, not Latino, not homosexual, to name only the more prominent ones — are repressed. Objective accomplishment carries little weight, correct credentials prevail. How did Soviet and Nazi universities differ? And with the future of the humanities and most of the social sciences now in the hands of the ideologists of caprice and special pleading, who can expect a future worthy of the disciplinary task?

Our future is upon us. To defend King's plagiarism, plagiarism finds itself cleaned up and made a virtue of blacks, as exemplified by the theories of Keith Miller of Arizona State University. As Pappas explains Miller's line of reasoning, "King's plagiarisms must have derived from his inability to separate himself from this [black] homiletic tradition [of borrowing sermons] and to comprehend the standards of an alien 'white' culture." The academy, therefore, must now redefine plagiarism to accommodate these "excluded" groups. So we have sunk to this! King does not deserve so shameful a defense. I believe Martin Luther King, Jr., was a man of conscience and character — but flesh and blood, like the rest of us. Those who thought to protect his name through deceit have traduced the man's own highest ideals, and did so, by excusing the inexcusable, in a way that ultimately diminished the stature and impoverished the heritage of a great man.

Nor can we readily distinguish between those who make excuses for plagiarists of a particular race or class and those who justify the exclusion of one race or class from the opportunities offered by an open society. Racism is racism, whether practiced by Nazis against Jews, by whites against blacks, or by blacks against whites, and the stigmata of racism, defending in the other what one would not tolerate in oneself, finding reasons for the lapses of the lesser sorts — these evils abound in the controversy narrated in this book. King's condescending defenders, not his critics, are the racists.

The intellect always contains within itself the power of its own renewal; reason does endure autonomous of the social order; persuasion compels, and argument changes minds. So the present corruption of intellect and its principal institutions cannot continue for very long. A hundred years from now, when issues other than race will perforce occupy this country of ours, what will people remember of the sorry record set forth here? I hope that someone will remember, in those days, that there was a man of sufficiently clear vision to see what counted: "It was Boston University's reputation, not Mr. King's, that was riding on the committee's handling of this controversy. We all know what King did, both good and bad; the only question was whether B.U. as an institution devoted to the pursuit of truth would have the honesty and integrity to admit its mistakes and acknowledge King's wrongdoing." In those few pure and simple phrases Pappas states all that the academy is supposed to represent. What a compliment he pays to us: "pursuit of truth . . . honesty and integrity . . . admit mistakes . . . acknowledge wrongdoing." Where else in our society do people address such expectations?

My own experience through a long academic career has taught this simple lesson: truth-telling is sometimes tough but always free of costs, but lying — though easy to accomplish — exacts an awful charge. I would not want it said, a century from now, that there was no one willing to stand by Theodore Pappas in his advocacy of the integrity of the academy and equal treatment of the races. That is why I am proud to invite readers to his book, and so to take my place beside the man possessed of the integrity to state, "In better days the follies of our heroes did not move us to subvert the moral underpinnings of our culture."

Those who share memories of an earlier age and understand the effect of the phrase "Senator, have you no shame?" will hear the echo today: "Professor, have you no shame?" And remembering the sounds of another day they will know what has changed — and what has stayed the same.

Jacob Neusner
Distinguished Research Professor of Religious Studies,
University of South Florida
Life Member of Clare Hall, Cambridge University

INTRODUCTION

The first edition of this book presented a series of documents and articles that traced every aspect of the King plagiarism story, from cover-up to whitewash. This revised and expanded edition of the book, though broader in scope, also approaches the King plagiarism tale in a chronological fashion, but it integrates the relevant documents and articles from the first edition into a narrative format. The articles reprinted herein appear with permission, and every effort has been made to reduce any repetition of the story line. A much abbreviated version of Chapter One appeared as the introduction to the first edition; portions of Chapter Two appeared in the January 1991 issue of *Chronicles: A Magazine of American Culture*, a publication of The Rockford Institute in Rockford, Illinois. Portions of Chapter Four appeared in the April and June 1991 issues of *Chronicles*; the book reviews in Chapter Five appeared in the November 1992 issue of *Chronicles*; and portions of Chapter Six appeared in the March and September 1993 issues of *Chronicles*. I thank Thomas Fleming, the editor of *Chronicles* and current president of The Rockford Institute, and Allan Carlson, the president of The Rockford Institute during my prime coverage of this story, for allowing me to tell this controversial but important tale. I also thank Charles Hallberg, the publisher of this new edition, for his kindness and generosity and, most importantly, for not gracing me with rejection number 41.

CHAPTER ONE

PLAGIARISM AND THE CULTURE WAR

"Some books are written for the pleasure or the zest of it. Other books are written as a painful duty, because there is something that needs to be said — and because other people have better sense than to say it."[1] Thomas Sowell's introductory remarks to *Civil Rights: Rhetoric or Reality?* (1984) aptly describe the following book. As I explained in the first edition published in 1994, there could be no more thankless enterprise or reckless pursuit, no endeavor more potentially destructive of personal and professional ties, than a critical study of an American hero such as Martin Luther King, Jr. But as readers of the first edition realize, this book, in many respects, has less to do with King and his legacy, with what he did and did not do, than with larger cultural issues, such as the politicization of the academy, the ethics of the press, the effect of our obsession with multiculturalism and diversity, and the sorry state of American publishing; such is the case with this updated and expanded edition of the book.[2]

Charles Sykes, Roger Kimball, Arthur Schlesinger, Jr., James Davison Hunter, Richard Bernstein, Mary Lefkowitz, Christopher Lasch, and a host of others, liberal and conservative alike, have well chronicled the excess, deception, and indoctrination that are both by-products and conduits of the so-called Culture War, and in this regard the following story is yet another sign of our degenerate times.[3] Lies, distortions, and the specious rationalizations that so often now pass for news and scholarship;

multiculturalism, political correctness, and the fashionable chatter about tolerance, inclusion, pluralism, and diversity — all play a part in the following tale, and all expose their true colors in the process. But the King plagiarism story is also different from any other chapter in the Culture War, making it a difficult and sensitive tale to recount. For it begins with the malfeasance of an American hero, and it is never pleasant to read about, never easy to discuss, a champion's feet of clay.

When French journalist Bernard Violet suggested in *Cousteau: A Biography* (1992) that the Grand Old Man of the Sea fell short of our vision of the sainted scientist — that some of Jacques Cousteau's movies had been secretly staged in a Marseilles studio, that divers had faked illnesses and equipment failure for dramatic effect, and that animals had been purposely harmed to induce a desired response for the camera — he touched off a firestorm of debate and controversy in his country. What is relevant here is how Violet felt upon uncovering such inglorious information about a man whom he and his countrymen have long revered as a national icon. In fact, the shock and disappointment he experienced are similar to what Clayborne Carson, the editor of the King Papers Project at Stanford University, reportedly felt upon learning that Martin Luther King, Jr., was a plagiarist. "I had admired Cousteau since the age of seven," says Violet, "when my father took me to see *Le monde du silence*, Cousteau's first film and winner of the Cannes Film Festival in 1956. Now I feel like an orphan."[4]

Orphans are often found in the wake of famous plagiarism scandals, and the disillusionment they experience is nothing to take lightly, as I learned firsthand. The occasion was a Chicago talk-radio show in the fall of 1990. I was being interviewed about my first article on King's plagiarized dissertation, which at the time was the only published work to describe in detail how and what King had pilfered. My argument was twofold: that King's personal courage and heroic leadership of the civil rights movement are beyond dispute, but his blatant plagiarizing in pursuit of America's highest academic degree — specifically, his stealing of large sections of a dissertation by Jack Boozer — was an indefensible act that should warrant the revocation of his Ph.D.; and that Boston University could posthumously award King an honorary doctorate for his contribution to civil rights but that it had an obligation as an institution devoted to the pursuit of truth to revile and revoke what was inappropriately earned. One female caller's response: "People like you should be 'taken out'!" And she did not mean to dinner and a movie.

When scholars first detected King's plagiarisms in 1987, it was still possible to defend proudly and with impunity the traditional definition of plagiarism and the commonsensical delineation of scholarly standards and responsibilities. Take, for example, Peter Shaw's 1982 essay on "Plagiary" in the *American Scholar*. His contention and conclusion were simple and straightforward and reflected the general conception of literary theft that had held sway for two centuries: that "as Lord Chesterfield pithily phrased it in the eighteenth century, a plagiarist is 'a man that steals other people's thoughts and puts 'em off for his own'"; that "literary critics and scholars must bear the responsibility to affirm that there is indeed such a thing as plagiarism and that they are capable of identifying it if necessary"; and that "the attempt to evade professional responsibility when a case of plagiarism arises only makes for further complications."[5] Thomas Mallon echoed these traditionalist views in *Stolen Words: Forays into the Origins and Ravages of Plagiarism* (1989).[6]

But when the King plagiarism story broke in late 1990 and received serious scrutiny over the next two years, traditional cultural norms were under intense attack. Contrary to what conservatives and traditionalists had predicted, postmodernism and deconstructionism did not remain mere parlor games of Susan Sontag and of the desk-bound class but rather spread in the guise of their nefarious offspring — multiculturalism, cultural relativism, political correctness and their many manifestations, from sensitivity seminars and diversity training to the war of defamation on the cultural inheritance of old Europe, on the Anglo-American traditions of our country, and on white Western males and their achievements in general — and tinctured every area of American culture: classrooms, boardrooms, and newsrooms alike. A "censorship of fashion," what Antonio Gramsci termed a "cultural hegemony," had been imposed on the apparatus of society — the schools, the arts, and the many mediums of public discourse, from television and textbooks to advertising and films — rejuvenating in the process the social rebels without a cause since the 1960's and 70's. It was at this very time — amid the assault on Western Civ. courses and the classics of Western literature; amid the rise of "hate crimes" and collegiate "speech codes"; amid the first serious push for girl Boy Scouts and gay Marines; amid the Supreme Court's extension of tax-exempt status and First Amendment protections to black-clad, spell-casting covens of witches and to the blood-drinking, animal-sacrificing worshippers of Babalu; amid the defense of rap lyrics espousing rape and murder as "a vital expression of an oppressed class"; amid the public funding of the "art" of Robert Mapplethorpe and his whip, Andres Serrano and his urine, and Karen Finley and her vegetables, pudding, and probes — it was amid this cultural orgy of absurdity that the King plagiarism story broke.

Defending time-honored Western customs and traditions — now deemed racist, sexist, tyrannical, and obsolete — had suddenly become verboten in polite circles if not downright injurious to one's career and social standing, and woe to the students who continued to believe that the only dumb question was the question never asked. The "radical chic" — our self-appointed arbiters of public standards and taste — seemingly held sway unencumbered, as the very institutions historically responsible for guarding truth and exposing falsehood — the academy and the press — surrendered all interest in such troubling tasks. Champions of traditional literary and academic mores now stood in stark contrast to the scores of writers, scholars, deans, and publishers who had hopped on the p.c. bandwagon, abandoned their roles as critics and watchdogs, forgone the unpleasantness of upholding propriety, and opted instead for a kinder and gentler conception of plagiarism that facilitated life for poacher and critic alike. Like profane books, depraved movies, and decadent art, plagiarism was on the verge of becoming yet another sacred cow that only simpletons, reactionaries, and self-righteous prigs would dare denounce. For according to this "new thinking" about literary theft, plagiarism must go the way of other taboos that have been modified and redefined in deference to sensitivity and social progress; plagiarism had become a battlefield for fighting the Culture War.

To appreciate the gravity of the following story, it is important to understand that plagiarism is a serious and growing problem; that the recent push to redefine plagiarism is directly tied to the politics of race and multiculturalism and to the popular belief that it is necessary to embrace a variety of moral views, no matter how incompatible, to uphold the rights and needs of minorities; and that the refusal to deal adequately with cases of plagiarism not only threatens to undermine our conceptions of authorship and originality on which Western scholarship and composition have been based for two centuries, but it reflects our culture's increasingly casual attitude toward individual responsibility and moral accountability.

The Nagging Problem of Plagiarism

When Vice Admiral Bobby Ray Inman announced on January 18, 1994, his decision not to pursue confirmation as Secretary of Defense, he repeated Robert Massie's old charge that William Safire is a plagiarist, saying this "does not, in my judgment, put [Safire] in a position to frame moral judgment on any of us, in or out of public service."[7] The battle that ensued between Safire and Inman on the one hand and between Safire and Massie on the other dragged on for months and included ad hominem attacks launched from *Nightline*, *The Nation*, and the *New York Times*. And though the real issue was not whether Safire is a plagiarist — but whether he had aided and abetted one by distributing an unpublished manuscript by Massie to another writer who ravaged it for an article in *Esquire* — this high-profile caterwauling made one thing clear: plagiarism has become one of the nagging problems of our day.

That plagiarism is relevant to our times can hardly be disputed. Senator Joseph Biden lost his bid for the presidency in 1987 when the press discovered that he had not only cribbed a paper at Syracuse Law School in 1965 but had more recently plagiarized the speeches of Neil Kinnock, John and Robert Kennedy, and Hubert Humphrey; in a less than graceful retreat, Biden then plagiarized his public apology for his plagiary, ripping off Tom Joad's famous lines ("wherever they's a fight . . . I'll be there") from *The Grapes of Wrath*. A 1990-1991 study by Donald McCabe of the Center for Academic Integrity indicated that over a third of undergraduates now admittedly plagiarize. "Plagiarism and Theft of Ideas" was the exclusive topic of the June 1993 conference of the American Association for the Advancement of Science. An article by Trudy Lieberman in the July/August 1995 issue of the *Columbia Journalism Review* reported that virtually every major newspaper in the country — from the *Los Angeles Times*, the *Washington Post*, and the *New York Times* to the *Denver Post*, the *Orlando Sentinel*, the *Chicago Sun-Times*, and the *St. Louis-Dispatch* — had recently fired or suspended an editorialist, a reporter, or news bureau chief for plagiarism. Steven Spielberg was dubbed "Steven Stealberg" by *Time* last November when it reported that the star movie director had been hit with a $10-million plagiarism suit for reportedly stealing the idea for the movie *Amistad* from a little-known historical novelist named Barbara Chase-Riboud, whose novel about the 19th-century slave revolt, *Echo of Lions*, had supposedly been presented to Spielberg's company, and separately to the sole screenwriter of Spielberg's film, years earlier but "rejected." It was then revealed that Ms. Chase-Riboud had plagiarized a history text for her 1986 novel *Valide*. And when listening to any contemporary movie sound track or Broadway theme song, it is difficult not to hear more than a faint echo of Wagner, Tchaikovsky, Gershwin, or Holst.[8]

Plagiarism is skyrocketing through cyberspace, where within seconds, with the push of a few buttons, students and scholars and novelists and hacks can cut and paste sections from disparate sources that once would have taken months if not years to collect. When it was discovered in August 1996 that a *Washington Post* book review by Jim Sleeper had been copied by an underling at the *San Francisco Chronicle*, it was a computer that received the brunt of the blame. According to the young reviewer, once he had downloaded Sleeper's work for "research purposes," the computer just somehow erased his work, leaving his byline above Sleeper's review. Sleeper was unconvinced. "While I don't have any reason to presume plagiarism," he said, "there's a level of incompetence and dereliction here that's unbelievable." But as explained by Michael Kinsley, the editor of the online magazine *Slate*, "Yes, it's easier to plagiarize in cyberspace. It's also easier to get caught." Kinsley's point was proven in late 1996, when an article by Katha Pollitt on the best-seller *The Rules* appeared in *Slate* and one John Naughton stole a verbatim chunk from it for his own article about the book in the London *Observer*. The *Observer's* editor apologized for the plagiarism and sent Pollitt a check for $1,000. [9]

Not all publications are as fair-minded and forthcoming as the *Observer*. When *Vanity Fair* columnist Christopher Hitchens stole passages from the first edition of this book for his May 1996 article on plagiarism, *Vanity Fair* refused not only to apologize for the theft but to publish any of the letters it received from readers who had noticed Hitchens' sleight-of-hand. In fact, *Vanity Fair* was more concerned with the accuracy of the filcher's aim than with the filcher or his filching. In a scene worthy of a *Monty Python* skit, the magazine's fact-checker even called and asked me to confirm the accuracy of the paragraphs that Hitchens would be stealing. When asked about his theft by Jay Stowe of the *New York Observer*, which picked up on the bizarre story, Hitchens praised my work on plagiarism ("Jolly good") and then gladly acknowledged stealing it for himself: "It [Pappas's work] enabled me to write my own piece . . . it's certain that I got [my information] from him. . . . I'm in favor of plagiarism and always have been. Wouldn't be able to write without it." [10] This from the man whose hobby was vilifying Mother Teresa as a "ghoul."

But if Hitchens is incapable of an original thought or work, he is not alone. For plagiarism scandals and controversies have embroiled some of the most popular writers and celebrated authors in recent years, such as Alex Haley, for his Pulitzer Prize-winning *Roots*; Dee Brown, for *Bury My Heart at Wounded Knee*; Gail Sheehy, for *Passages*; Ken Follett, for *The Key to Rebecca*; Norman Mailer, for his first book on Marilyn Monroe; Jacob Epstein, for *Wild Oats*; Joe McGinniss, for *The Last Brother*; David

Leavitt, for *While England Sleeps*; Stephen Oates, for his biographies of Abraham Lincoln, William Faulkner, and Martin Luther King, Jr.; Bruno Bettelheim, for *The Uses of Enchantment: The Meaning and Importance of Fairy Tales*; Maya Angelou, for her "Inaugural Poem"; TM Guru Deepak Chopra, for *Ageless Bodies, Timeless Mind*; Ismael Kadare, for *The Concert*; and journalist Ruth Shalit and columnist Molly Ivans.[11]

But despite this rampant poaching, some commentators continue to view plagiarism as much ado about nothing. James Kincaid, for instance, in the January 20, 1997, issue of *The New Yorker*, totes out the old chestnut about plagiarism being nothing more than imitation and a source of inspiration. He cites Aristotle ("All men delight in imitations") and Northorp Frye ("Poetry can only be made out of other poems; novels out of other novels") to chide the literary bluenoses who work themselves into a tizzy about "the report that your fifth grader lifted from the encyclopedia" and other "harmless acts, standard practice, unavoidable short trips into the common ground of language and thought."[12] There are three obvious objections to this specious bromide. First, the classical notion of imitation is too complicated to summarize in a five-word epigram from Aristotle, as will later be shown. Second, it is true that the creative process does not occur in a vacuum, as Leonard Meyer pointed out in *Music, the Arts, and Ideas*: "A work of art does not exist in isolated splendor. It is a part of history — the history of culture, the history of the art, and the history of the artist."[13] But let us go even further than Frye, Kincaid, or Meyer: there is arguably no story plot, theme, or human emotion that was not delineated by Homer in the *Odyssey* or the *Iliad*; there is no three-note progression that cannot be found in Bach; and since the time of Socrates, Plato, and Aristotle, there is nothing fundamentally new under the philosophical sun. Of course we are the children of parents — biologically and civilizationally — and we stand on the shoulders of the giants who walked before us. No one denies this. But it is one thing to admire, even to emulate, the slashes and dashes of a Vincent van Gogh; quite another to claim *Sunflowers* as your own work. Or as the Great Cham of Literature quipped, "An inferior genius may, without any imputation of servility, pursue the path of the ancients, provided he declines to tread in their footsteps."[14] If the current plague of plagiarism is any indication, we as a culture are not only treading in the footsteps of our betters, but have stolen their socks and shoes as well.

Third, a schoolboy's cribbing is indeed a "harmless act" in the grand scheme of things. But what sensible person would argue otherwise? Surely few scholars believed that the foundation of Western civilization was shaken in June 1980 when the University of Oregon plagiarized Stanford University's handbook on plagiarism, and certainly few composers who feel victimized by literary theft end up as a homicidal, mask-wearing maniac intent on seeking vengeance on an uncaring world, as Erik does in the 1943 film version of *The Phantom of the Opera*. But what a schoolboy's antics have to do with instances of grand verbal larceny, and why the former should mitigate the seriousness of the offense or cause a rethinking of the vice, let alone undercut our faith in our ability to detect such fraud, is not at all clear. Moreover, since when do we define acceptable behavior by the standards and missteps of children? By this logic, chop-shop operators should be treated with leniency because toddlers stealing candy are not forced into chain gangs.

No, plagiarism is not treason or serial murder. But as a form of cheating and as an act of mendacity, plagiarism is a serious offense (and a criminal offense as well, when violations of copyright and trademark are involved). For a plagiarist is like the two-bit thug who steals and wears a gentleman's eyepiece in order to put on airs: he commits a hybrid act of deviltry, combining theft, deception, and pretension. Because plagiarism smacks of the meretricious and ignoble, it reflects badly not only on the character of the plagiarist but on the character of the country that allows it to thrive and to take root in its culture; it speaks volumes about the country's educational system, literary establishment, and the state of its critical and creative faculties. Dante understood this "character issue," which is why he chose the formidable monster Geryon to represent fraud and to rule the falsifiers, thieves, and "all such filthy cheats" in the darker and deeper recesses of Hell. He held special disdain for miscreants of this sort because, unlike gluttons and hoarders and other persons guilty of mere incontinence, these sinners had perverted the divine gift of intelligence by which man can discover truth and used it to deceive for temporal gain. "Since fraud is the vice of which man alone is capable, God loathes it most."[15]

But plagiarism is also a kidnapping of sorts, both in emotional as well as etymological terms. *Plagiarius* was the Latin term for the kidnapping of slaves which the Roman poet Martial co-opted to describe the poaching of words. But more significantly, plagiarism has all the overtones of an actual kidnapping — of the stealing of something sired, something precious and irreplaceable — as Thomas Mallon explained in *Stolen Words*:

> Think how often, after all, a writer's books are called his children. To see the writer's words kidnapped, to find them imprisoned, like changelings, on someone else's equally permanent page, is to become vicariously absorbed by violation.[16]

This sense of violation does not faze Kincaid. In fact, not even serious instances of fraud concern him, because "the authorities can take care of the few [plagiarists] who cause pain."[17]

If only this were so. For as this book makes clear, the problem today is not only that the "authorities" are not dealing with this increase in malfeasance but that many of the "authorities" are frauds and miscreants themselves. The question is no longer how many watchdogs are needed for our protection, but rather *quis custodiet ipsos custodes* — who will watch the watchdogs.

Fraud and plagiarism in the literary, scientific, and scholarly worlds are simply more prominent and prolific than generally realized, and the way in which many cases of impropriety have been ignored, whitewashed, and covered up by the press, by editors, by publishers, and by universities has only aggravated the problem and encouraged such perfidy. For example, one of the most embarrassing plagiarism scandals to shake the literary world in recent years went virtually undiscussed. When Ballantine Books announced in 1994 that Indrani Aikath-Gyaltsen, the "promising" novelist who had committed suicide the year before, had plagiarized her widely acclaimed novel *Cranes' Morning* from Elizabeth Goudge's 1956 novel *The Rosemary Tree*, the literary world's collective jaw fell with a deafening thud. It seems Aikath-Gyaltsen, who was born in India but educated in the United States, had merely changed the story's setting from England to her native land, inserted Hindu for Christianity wherever appropriate in the text, and then purloined virtually verbatim whatever was left. The Goudge estate in England was so incensed that it pressed Ballantine not only for a public condemnation of the plagiarism but for a worldwide recall of all copies of the fraudulent work.

Most embarrassing was the way in which the literary establishment had lavishly praised Aikath-Gyaltsen. Before the plagiarism had been detected, *Publishers Weekly* had gushed that the young woman "dissects domestic life with the gimlet precision of Jane Austen." The *New York*

Times had called her novel "magic," "full of humor and insight," with "a
countryside you suspect you may have visited before." The *Washington
Post* cried "exquisite," a book "at once achingly familiar and breathtak-
ingly new." "Achingly familiar," "a countryside you suspect you may have
visited before" — indeed.[18]

When the unfortunate news broke, Eastern publishers, editors, and
critics were appalled at the "brazenness" of this literary cutpurse, but was
it really the brazenness that bothered them or just the yolk dripping from
their faces? For too busy professing their shock and consternation, they
had entirely missed (or were too chagrined to discuss) the moral of this
story: a second-rate novel that was originally panned by the critics as
little more than a penny dreadful when it was originally published in the
1950's had become a monumental work of literature 40 years later once
plagiarized and set in a Third World country. The decline of the novel,
the deterioration of standards, an obsession with diversity, an infatuation
with the Third World, the self-flagellation that today passes for tolerance
and sensitivity — herein lie a tale about much more than mere plagiarism.

Nor was plagiarism the sole story when the queen of Harlequin romance novels was caught lifting the bodice of another romance novelist's
work. As David Streitfeld reported in the *Washington Post* on July 30,
1997, some of the throbbing loins and heaving bosoms from Janet Dailey's
90-plus novels (over 300 million copies sold) have come from the pages
of a younger rival, Nora Roberts. But apparently the plagiarism was not
Dailey's fault. Flip Wilson used to say, "The Devil made me do it," but in
this case blame rested with a psychological disorder. Her problem, said
her attorney, was "hypomania," a disorder caused from the stress of a
miscarriage, a failed in vitro fertilization, a father with cancer, and a
mother who had brain surgery. As Dailey explained, her "essentially ran-

dom and non-pervasive acts of copying are attributable to a psychological problem that I never even suspected I had. I have already begun treatment for the disorder and have been assured that, with treatment, this behavior can be prevented in the future." Dailey's publicist in Los Angeles added that the plagiarism also stemmed from stress associated with the grieving process: the novelist's dog had died as well.[19]

There are many lessons to be learned from this literary legerdemain, especially from the pilfering now common among the pundits and policywonks of the Beltway. Take, for example, the case of Joe Cobb, the Heritage Foundation's John M. Olin Senior Fellow in Political Economy. Paul Gigot of the *Wall Street Journal* had assured his readers in a May 5, 1994, column that the Clinton-backed proposal of a World Trade Organization posed no threat to American sovereignty because the "independent" trade expert of the "opposition" party had analyzed it and declared it safe and sound. "Mr. Cobb," wrote Gigot, "the GOP economist who's studied the GATT text, says, yes [to the WTO], because the WTO is no threat to American self-rule. . . . He says he'd shutter both the World Bank and International Monetary Fund if he could, but the WTO is different." What Gigot apparently did not know is that Cobb's "independent" analysis was a virtual duplication of a study by the Advisory Committee for Trade Policy and Negotiations (ACTPN). Whole sections of Cobb's "assessment" had been lifted from ACTPN'S work. Composed primarily of corporate and banking interests, ACTPN had been hired by President Clinton's Trade Representative and had produced its study by government contract. In other words, under the guise of an "independent analyst" for the "opposition" party, the Republicans were marketing the Democrats' agenda, which of course was the same as their own.[20]

Something similar happened the following year, when the Cato Institute, a libertarian think-tank known for its opposition to environmental regulations, issued a brief on the North American Free Trade Agreement that looked strangely similar to an analysis of the agreement made and released earlier by trade lawyers Kenneth Berlin and Jeffrey M. Lang. Numerous mainstream environmentalist groups had hired the latter to write a favorable analysis of NAFTA to sell to skeptical lawmakers on Capitol Hill.[21]

Instead of exploring the implications of such shenanigans — what they say about our political class and how they bring into question whether any significant differences still exist between our two major political parties — the mainstream media simply ignored them. And when a media organ did allude to either story, it only did so as an amusing aside, as one of the news weeklies did with regard to Joe Cobb's plagiarisms, entitling its *two-sentence* article on the incident, "Conservative Copycats."

Republicans were embarrassed further when "Mr. Virtue" himself, William Bennett, was caught in two controversies involving literary deception. The first occurred in January 1995, when Bennett read a prepared statement before the House Appropriations Subcommittee on Interior and Related Matters calling for the abolishment of the National Endowment for the Arts and the National Endowment for the Humanities. The House committee assumed that Bennett was speaking about his own experience and observations as director of NEH in the 1980's. Bennett recounted the difficulties he experienced in trying to establish a program that would promote traditional works of philosophy. "By the third year," he said,

> it was obvious that this program was going the way of all the others. The books were being Marxized, feminized, decon-

structed and politicized. High-school teachers, far from exposed to "the best which has been taught and said in the world," were being indoctrinated in the prevailing dogmas of academia.[22]

As reported by Al Kamen in the *Washington Post*, this passage "tracks" the remarks of historian Gertrude Himmelfarb in an article in *Commentary*. "Track" is one of the many kind and gentle euphemisms for plagiarism, and this portion of Bennett's statement was a verbatim excerpt from Professor Himmelfarb's essay.

Bennett said he had never seen the article in *Commentary*. As he later explained, Professor Himmelfarb had included this passage in a statement that she had intended to read before the same House committee. When she decided not to appear, she reportedly "gave me [Bennett] her testimony and told me to use it as I saw fit . . . and she asked me not to cite it."[23] Now, Bennett was not technically guilty of plagiarism, because he supposedly had received permission to use Professor Himmelfarb's work. But permission doth not a virtuous act make. The general feeling was that a high-profile moralizer should not be passing off the words of others as his own and then declaring, once tripped up in the deception, "I was told I could do it."

The second controversy involved Bennett's best-seller *The Book of Virtues*, which as *The New Yorker* exposed in February 1995 was really written and edited by someone other than Bennett: by one of Bennett's former speechwriters, John Cribb. As the magazine explained, Bennett did not have enough money to pay the young scribe: "Not to put too fine a point on it, [Bennett] was suffering from a small cash-flow embarrassment: he had long ago spent the advance on his two-book deal with Simon & Schuster. Being a great man, though, William had an idea: if John would stick with the project for a year, William would give John about a third of any profits that the resulting 'Book of Virtues' earned."[24] Thus did Bennett get the young man to ghostwrite the book for him.

Ghostwriting is an age-old method of publishing for the rich and unlettered, and without it America would never have had a Pulitzer Prize-winning "author" become President. But no political figure has ever had a ghostwritten book as widely popular and profitable as Bill Bennett's, and so it was inevitable that *The New Yorker's* story would raise questions about Bennett's credibility and sincerity. For the impression was now that the book derived not from a public servant long troubled by the moral direction of the country but instead from a hired hack who by peddling virtue helped his boss to fulfill his two-book contract and made millions of dollars for both of them in the process. Of course, this revelation did not negate the book's usefulness, or even its "virtues," but it did — together with the deceptive testimony given before the House — color the public's impression of Bennett as a defender of standards, ethics, and morality. As *The New Yorker* sniffed, "Virtue is its own reward, especially when you figure in foreign-language royalties and subsidiary rights."[25]

Campus Follies

If the mainstream media are loath to treat plagiarism scandals as anything more significant than fodder for gossip, the academic community — and its professional associations, as will later be shown — is inclined to ignore them altogether. Historian Stephen Nissenbaum spent years trying to convince both publishers and universities that his book *Sex, Diet, and Debility in Jacksonian America* had been brazenly plagiarized by a young historian at Texas Tech named Jayme Sokolow. As Nissenbaum wrote in the March 28, 1990, issue of the *Chronicle of Higher Education*, "though Mr. Sokolow's activities first came to light nine years ago . . . not one of the institutions that have learned of them has openly condemned what he did. That includes two universities, at least seven publishing houses, and three major national organizations."[26] Though Professor Nissenbaum finally succeeded in publicizing the theft, students can still find Sokolow's *Eros and Modernization* right alongside Nissenbaum's book in the library: the two works are now shelved together because of the "similarity" of their topics.

Oxford University spent virtually the entire year of 1994 dealing with plagiarism scandals that resulted in the revocation of three academic degrees, including one from a Unitarian minister who had killed his wife. Until then, Oxford had rescinded only one other degree because of plagiarism *this century*. Perhaps the most interesting of the three cases for Americans was the widespread pilfering of historian Gary Owens Hughes, who had plagiarized his Trinity College doctorate from a dissertation written at Princeton. Impressed by what the *Philadelphia Inquirer* called his "pearl-like diction" (read: British accent) and "golden" credentials, Temple University had hired Hughes and brought him to the United States in 1987 to help write its multivolume *Biographical Dictionary of Early Pennsylvania Legislators*. But when scores of his plagiarized articles began popping up in journals on both sides of the Atlantic the following year, he was fired; it was not until 1994, however, that Oxford revoked Hughes's doctorate. Said Dr. Kenneth Wilson, principal at Westminster College: "Matters like this have to be taken seriously. It's absolutely essential for the future of academic life. Plagiarism is climbing on the back of other people."[27]

But even university administrators, ostensibly the "authorities" whom James Kincaid had in mind for policing literary fraud and theft, have been caught "climbing on the back of other people." Take the case of H. Joachim Maitre, who as dean of Boston University's College of Communication gave a 1991 Commencement Address that focused on how Hollywood and television glorify the ugly and the beautiful at the expense of religion and traditional values; many called the speech moving and powerful. There was only one problem: Dean Maitre had taken large sections of the speech virtually verbatim from an article by film critic Michael Medved. Considering that Medved's article had already appeared in the *Wall Street Journal* and *Reader's Digest* — two more widely circulated publications could hardly be found — the dean's actions left commentators wondering whether plagiarism constituted the real offense. As a character suggests in C.P. Snow's novel *The Affair*, which deals with a case of scientific fraud, "there are times when stupidity seems to me the greater crime."[28]

But there were two intriguing upshots to the Maitre contretemps. First, the *New York Time's* coverage of the story was written by its Boston bureau chief, one Fox Butterfield. Save for a few sentences rearranged and a word changed here and there, Mr. Butterfield's report had a striking resemblance to a story about Maitre that ran in the *Boston Globe*. The penalty for plagiarizing a piece about plagiarism? A one-week suspension.[29]

Second, the Maitre affair followed on the heals of the King plagiarism scandal, and the disparate way in which Boston University handled each controversy did not go unnoticed. As Patrick Buchanan noted in his nationally syndicated column,

> What makes the ducking of this [King plagiarism] issue so revealing a case of intellectual cowardice is that recently B.U. let go its dean of communications, Joachim Maitre. His crime? An East German refugee and fierce anti-communist, Maitre gave a commencement address in which he failed to attribute passages borrowed from a piece by critic Michael Medved. . . . Yet, the *Boston Globe*, in 12 stories in 12 days, stirred up a faculty mob

[against Maitre], giving ample space to its anonymous quotes. We await the *Globe*'s campaign to strip the title of "Dr." from Dr. King.[30]

Another high-ranking administrator caught in a plagiarism scandal was Brigham Young University President Merrill J. Bateman. In his Inaugural Address in April 1996, Bateman delivered a speech on moral relativism which just happened to use lines from an article in the January 1996 issue of *First Things*, written by the same source whom William Bennett had tapped, Gertrude Himmelfarb. When *Sunstone*, a magazine of Mormon studies, exposed the plagiarism, President Bateman quickly apologized — not for the plagiarism, but for the "ambiguity." In fact, Batment focused attention not on his actions but on the "confusion" of the whistleblower. As he convolutedly explained, "What had been presented in the accusatory article as disjointed sentences without attribution were consecutive sentences in one paragraph plus the first part of a second. . . . What confused the [whistleblower] was [an unacknowledged] citation directly followed a short phrase placed inside quotation marks." Scott Abbott of BYU's Germanic and Slavic Department rightly cut to the larger issue: the president's plagiarism was bad enough, but "the big problem is that he hasn't read the primary texts." (One also wonders whether admitting to an inability to use quotation marks is really the best defense for a university president.)[31]

The academy has also had problems policing fraud and plagiarism in the hard sciences. We have tended to view scientists since the Civil War as paragons of objectivity and as champions of truth who are selfless in motivation, dispassionate in research, and immune to the lure of coin and convention. Just how often this image falls short of reality is now painfully clear. For example, the investigations of Walter Stewart and

Ned Feder of the National Institutes of Health in the 1980's were indispensable in uncovering the extent of the transgressions of John Darsee of
the Harvard Medical School, the widely acclaimed rising star of biomedi-
cal research who, after publishing 122 journal articles in a little over two
years, was found to have faked data in nearly every paper.[32]

Harvard's scientific community has been especially hard hit by fraud
and plagiarism controversies in recent years. After the Darsee scandal
came the Scheffer C. G. Tseng affair of 1986, in which Harvard dilly-
dallied in releasing a researcher at one of its infirmaries who was conducting unauthorized tests on humans with an experimental drug. Tseng and
his supervisor, associate professor Kenneth Kenyon, just happened to have
owned stock in the company manufacturing the drug, the sales of which
had reportedly netted Tseng a million dollars by the time of his release. A
third case involved one of Harvard Medical School's leading psychia-
trists, Shervert Frazier, who was exposed as a plagiarist in 1988. As Morton
Hunt wrote in the *New York Times Magazine*, a scandal like this is particularly loathsome "not only because it violates the scientific ethic of truth-
fulness but because prestige, position and grant money are largely dependent on the originality and quantity of one's publications."[33]

But if prestige, position, and grant money are dependent on originality
and therefore act as curbs on fraud and plagiarism in the sciences, they
just as often act as catalysts of such vice. This seems especially true of the
scientific misconduct now raging throughout the Far East, especially in
China, where a half-dozen serious scandals have occurred since 1993. In
fact, the malfeasance has become so common that both *Science* and the
Chinese Scientific News have regular rubrics for reporting on the Chinese
shenanigans of the month. One of the plagiarists turned out to be Chen
Zhangliang, China's most prominent young molecular biologist and the

vice president of Peking University. As a researcher explained to *Science*, "Some Chinese scientists think that they can't compete equally in Western journals because of a problem with English. So they like to copy what others have done and then fill in what is new." Regarding Dr. Chen, the researcher concluded: "I think he's part of the new generation that is pushing to adopt Western standards." If Dr. Chen's plagiarisms are any indication, he should have no problem adopting to Western "standards."[34]

Also noteworthy was the dispute between two epidemiologists at the University of Hong Kong, which finally resulted in 1994, after seven years of litigation costing 16 million Hong Kong dollars, in what *Nature* magazine called "the world's first legal verdict in which a scientist has been found guilty of plagiarism." The case involved the plagiarizing of a questionnaire that a team of scientists had developed for researching lung cancer in female nonsmokers, which is not, as researcher Takeshi Hirayama explained, a petty offense. For "success or failure of a [multimillion-dollar] study depends on the quality of the questionnaire."[35]

On May 1, 1995, a federal court jury in Maryland ruled against the University of Alabama (Birmingham) and four of its researchers accused of copping the work of a researcher at Cornell University and then incorporating it into a grant proposal. The aggrieved party was awarded $2 million in damages. As Nathaniel J. Pallone and James J. Hennessy explained in *Fraud and Fallible Judgment: Varieties of Deception in the Social and Behavioral Sciences* (1995), what made this case significant was that the victim, as in the Hong Kong case described above, sought redress not through the oversight channels in place in academia, in which scholars increasingly have little faith, but through the courts: "The case has been widely interpreted as a portent of things to come unless the scientific enterprise, and its myriad component disciplines, shows itself both willing and able to rigorously police misconduct within its own ranks."[36]

Marcel C. LaFollette had highlighted this very problem in *Stealing into Print: Fraud, Plagiarism, and Misconduct in Scientific Publishing* (1992). She showed how the peer-review process and political grandstanding have hindered attempts to crack down on fraud and plagiarism in the sciences and noted that the latter is now the more prevalent form of malfeasance: "Both the NSF [National Science Foundation] and NIH [National Institutes of Health] now report that they investigate substantially more allegations involving plagiarism and stolen ideas than allegations involving falsified or altered data."[37]

The Whistleblower

When in Rex Stout's *Plot It Yourself* Nero Wolfe's assistant interrogates a literary agent about a case of "plagiarism upside down" — the planting of a back-dated manuscript of a published work for purposes of blackmailing the legitimate author as a plagiarist — he senses "from [the agent's] tone that anyone who made a plagiarism claim was a louse."[38] Here, in a nutshell, is the typical fate of the whistleblower. No one suffers the pangs and arrows of outrageous fortune like the exposer of a famous plagiarist, for it is he, not the sinner and certainly not the sin, who becomes the center of debate, the target of abuse, and the victim of the hot and harsh lights of public scrutiny.

This is especially true when the plagiarist is a person of color and the whistleblower is not. Take, for instance, the scandal last year in France over the plagiary of Franco-Cameroon writer Colixthe Beyala, who received the *grand prix du roman* from the French Academy in October 1996 for her plagiarized work *Les honneurs perdus*. Though no one denied that Beyala was a plagiarist, more criticism was leveled against the whistleblowers than against the "writer." In fact, anyone denouncing her larceny and defending literary standards was branded a hate-mongering member of the fascist fringe. "It appears," wrote Pierre Assouline in the February 1997 issue of *Lire*, "that to denounce her plagiarism would be to play into the hands of the [far-right] National Front. It's crazy!" What particularly galled him was that Beyala even has a history of plagiarism; she was found guilty by a court in May 1996 of having used "fraudulent copying" to compose one of her other books, *Le petit prince de Belleville*. The young woman's defense? As Michel Richard wrote in the January 25, 1997, issue of *Le Point*, "Calixthe defends herself by claiming an extraordinary memory peculiar to the African tradition in which one may, without recrimination, resort to recycling a scene or anecdote from another source and, even more astonishingly, in which one may resolve oneself from any ill intention because she is a woman and a Black."[39]

The Colixthe Beyala affair is a prime example of how "when a plagiarism is detected," as Edgar Allan Poe noted, "it generally happens that the public sympathy is with the plagiarist."[40] Neal Bowers learned this the hard way. As he related in *Words for the Taking: The Hunt for a Plagiarist* (1997), upon discovering that a sociopathic plagiarist had copped and published under various pseudonyms scores of his poems in journals around the world — including one poignant poem which Bowers had written in memory of his dead father — he could find few colleagues or friends to sympathize with his plight and even fewer who would at least not blame *him* for his troubles. "Many of those from whom I expected support," he wrote, "took the part of the plagiarist, expressing concern for him as a misguided or tortured individual. Some accused me of laying false charges, some of being arrogant in the defense of my creative property, and some simply never responded to my call for help."[41]

Compared to this, Garry Wills of Northwestern University got off rather easy. Wills was one of the few high-profile scholars to state publicly that

King's blatant thievery was grounds for revoking his doctorate. In his chapter on King in *Certain Trumpets: The Call of Leaders* (1994), Wills admits that "the most famous of [King's] perorations ["I Have a Dream"] comes from another man, from Archibald Carey," but later adds:

> Normal as this kind of borrowing was among preachers, it is inexcusable in academic terms, and I believe [King's] doctorate should be rescinded by Boston University. (I also think John Kennedy's Pulitzer Prize, won in an even greater exercise of false pretense [for *Profiles in Courage*, which Theodore Sorensen and other aides have been accused of writing] should be rescinded — for one thing this would make judges of prizes and examiners of doctoral students more conscientious at their work.)[42]

What Wills did not tell the reader is that King principally plagiarized "white sources" — the work of liberal white writers, white preachers, white scholars — but that in the case of the "I Have a Dream" speech, King took, copyrighted, and later defended his legal right to the words and thoughts of another black man. Because the press and the academy act as though all blacks are alike, all blacks think alike, and all blacks supported King and the civil rights movement, they naturally conclude that Archibald Carey — ipso facto — must have felt honored to have his words stolen by someone of the stature of King. This may have been the case, but no evidence of this has ever been offered.[43]

It should also be pointed out that Professor Wills' bold call for the revocation of King's doctorate is not found in his long chapter on King in *Certain Trumpets* but rather in a footnote buried at the end of the book. If Wills did this in the hope that few would read this passage, or did it in propitiation for his sin of candor, the strategy failed. As Frank Kermode noted in this review of Wills' book in the *New York Times Book Review*, "[Wills] doesn't even suggest a posthumous honorary doctorate [for King] in its place."[44]

Walter Stewart and Ned Feder received harsher treatment. When they turned their attention (and their computerized method of detecting plagiarism) away from fraud in the sciences and began uncovering literary theft among celebrated scholars in the humanities, the heat quickly came down on them. On May 10, 1993, the NIH confiscated their computer files and terminal, forbad them to address the issue of plagiarism, and reassigned them to other duties before placing them on leave. "My partner was told," Stewart told the *Chicago Tribune*, "that it would be inappropriate for him to comment on any errors or problems he might see in published scientific literature. We think that's just what someone who monitors research projects funded with the government's [i.e., the taxpayers'] money ought to be doing."[45] And what precipitated this clampdown? It seems pressure was exerted on NIH via a tie to the Clinton administration, a person close to one of the scholars Stewart and Feder had recently investigated. A better example of political intrigue could hardly be found, and yet the story was buried.

This "burying" of the unpalatable and politically sensitive is not out of character for the neutered hounds of the corporate press. Thanks to Charles Babington's article "Embargoed" in the January 28, 1991, issue of the *New Republic*, reprinted in Chapter Three, we now know about the numerous publications that had long known about King's plagiarisms but deliberately suppressed the story.[46] *Chronicles: A Magazine of American Culture* and I first became interested in the King plagiarism story in mid-1990, when we heard 1) that a university had threatened to block a scholar's bid for tenure if he followed through with his plans to discuss King's plagiarisms, and 2) that the National Endowment for the Humanities, which has reportedly allocated more than a million dollars to the King Papers Project, had long known about King's plagiarisms but had yet to pressure Clayborne Carson and his staff for a prompt disclosure of the evidence. As Charles Babington noted, "Lynne Cheney and fellow [NEH] officials were not obligated to divulge the information. . . . And they didn't."

We became directly involved in the story in the spring of 1990, when we received, accepted, and set for publication a short article from John Shelton Reed, a professor of sociology at the University of North Carolina at Chapel Hill and a longtime contributing editor to *Chronicles*, that praised King and the civil rights movement but mildly rebuked him for plagiarizing his dissertation, which had been rumored about, especially in the NEH circles in which John Reed traveled, for quite some time but had not yet been publicly discussed. However, after sending an advance copy of his article to Boston University and receiving a stern letter in return, and upon learning that his discussion of King's plagiarisms might also violate the NEH's confidentiality rule, Reed got scared and begged us to kill his piece at the last minute, which we did. It was then — when faced with the possibility that this story and its serious implications were not going to be tackled by the academic community — that I ordered the two dissertations and examined the evidence for myself. One thing was now clear: the story had evolved beyond anything King might have done as a student.[47]

The Past Revisited

Berating the bearer of the bad news instead of dealing with the bad news itself is a feature common to famous plagiarism cases since the time of Coleridge. Why the age of Coleridge, the late 18th and early 19th centuries, is relevant to this discussion, and to the King plagiarism story in particular, might not be obvious without remembering when the idea of plagiarism first began to challenge the classical notion of imitation that had long reigned in the West as the preferred method of composition. As George Kennedy explains in *Classical Rhetoric and Its Christian and Secular Tradition from Ancient to Modern Times* (1980), classical writing and oratory were

> to a considerable extent a pastiche, or piecing together of commonplaces, long or short. . . . The student memorized passages as he would letters and made up a speech out of these elements as he would words out of letters. . . . In the Middle Ages handbooks of letter-writing often contained formulae, such as openings and closes, which the student could insert into a letter, and a whole series of formulary rhetorics existed in the Renaissance.[48]

Rhetoricians, however, expected these models, formulae, pastiches, and commonplaces to be recognized by their auditors and accepted for what they were — either clichés of basic oratory or time-honored excerpts from the masters that lent beauty and authority to their work. There was no attempt to deceive or to pass off the genius of others as one's own, which, of course, a plagiarist aims to do. As Seneca the Elder said of Ovid, "as he had done with many other lines of Virgil [he] borrowed the idea, not desiring to deceive people, but to have it openly recognized as borrowed."[49] And as Francis Meres said of Shakespeare, "As the soul of Euphorbus was thought to live in Pythagoras, so the sweet witty soul of Ovid lives in mellifluous and honey-tongued Shakespeare."[50]

This classical tradition of imitation was not significantly challenged until the 18th century. It was then that authorship, originality, and plagiarism became for the first time prime issues of debate, and by the age of Coleridge and Romanticism, an obsession with originality and a fanatical crediting of literary property had become defining features of Western culture. This development was not to everyone's liking. Tennyson was appalled by the "prosaic set growing up among us — editors of booklets, bookworms, index-hunters, or men of great memories . . . [that] will not allow one to say, 'Ring the bell' without finding that we have taken it from Sir P. Sidney, or even to use such a simple expression as the ocean 'roars' without finding out the precise verse in Homer or Horace from which we have plagiarized it."[51] This "prosaic set" that Tennyson, Pope, and others railed against was the new breed of scholar — the "pedants without insight, intellectuals without love" — who trivialized literature, distorted aesthetics, and sought prestige and honor not through originality but by impugning the originality of writers of proven talent.

The other factor contributing to this heightened concern for authorship stemmed from a socioeconomic, not aesthetic, change: the profitability of putting pen to pad had given rise to those Grub Street scribblers known as professional writers. It is not surprising, then, that the first detailed discussions and definitions of plagiarism — as well as an increased interest in the detection of forged documents and the first serious calls for copyright statutes — issue from this period and from the likes of Johnson, Pope, Goldsmith, and De Quincey. Thomas Mallon, in *Stolen Words*, described the transition this way:

> A modern world was printing and distributing itself into existence. Literary "careers" would be "made," and writerly goods would get sold, not because they were skillful variants of earlier ones but because they were original. . . . Eventually a bourgeois world would create its own new genre, the novel,

and authors would be brand names, the "new Scott" asked for
like this year's carriage model.[52]

The continuity between this period and our own in the handling of
famous cases of plagiarism can most readily be seen by juxtaposing two of the
most prominent plagiarists of the last two centuries: Samuel Taylor Coleridge
and Martin Luther King, Jr. That Coleridge boldly plagiarized — not in his
poems but in his *Biographia Literaria* and in his lectures on Shakespeare — is
still not widely known among the general public. What Peter Shaw wrote 16
years ago in the *American Scholar* remains largely true:

> Today the general reading public remains for the most part
> unaware that Coleridge was a plagiarist, while literary critics
> and professors of English — outside of those who specialize in
> the study of Romantic poetry — are largely unaware of the
> extent and significance of his plagiarism. The manner in which
> the present state of ignorance came about bears directly on the
> literary world's current unwillingness to deal with contempo-
> rary cases of plagiarism.[53]

Though these two men differ in ways that are as numerous as they are
obvious, their similarities as plagiarists are nevertheless striking and useful for highlighting how famous cases of pilfering typically play out. Both
men plagiarized some of their most influential prose and were publicly
exposed as pilferers only after death. The plagiarisms of both men were
widely rumored and whispered about prior to their exposure and were
secretly known by numerous individuals who suppressed the story. Both
men had spirited celebrants for whom no excuse, justification, or rationalization was too fantastic to enlist in the defense of their hero's work
and reputation. And both men publicly defended their purloined property as their own.

Take, for example, the arguments of Coleridge's principal defenders, which both Thomas Mallon and Peter Shaw have summarized. In rebutting J.C. Ferrier's relentless documentation of Coleridge's thefts, Thomas McFarland argued that "it is surprising and rather anticlimactic to find that when the firing is over Ferrier has discovered no more than nineteen pages of plagiarism in the hundreds that make up the *Biographia Literaria.*"[54] The committee that Boston University convened to investigate King's plagiarisms adopted a similar kind of argument in its September 1991 report. Because King stole "only" one third of his doctoral dissertation — 45 percent of the first half, 21 percent of the second — the thesis remains an "intelligent contribution to scholarship" and "no thought should be given to the revocation of Dr. King's doctoral degree."[55] As Peter Shaw wondered with regard to McFarland's defense, "If nineteen pages are anticlimactic, it is not clear what would have impressed McFarland in the circumstances — twenty-one pages copied? Twenty-five? Fifty?"[56] Similarly so with Boston University's exoneration of King. How much more would King have had to "borrow" to invite B.U.'s censure? Seventy-five percent? Eighty?

McFarland refers to Coleridge's "mode of composition — composition by mosaic organization." This language is similar to the rhetoric of Walter Jackson Bate and James Engell, who compared Coleridge's plagiarisms to a "chemical compound." But such phrases are merely euphemisms for plagiarism. They are typical of the rhetorical mufflers with which apologists for plagiarists swathe and bedizen themselves in an effort to suppress the cold reality of theft. At one point Clayborne Carson even forbad everyone involved with the King Papers Project to utter the dreaded "p-word." He spoke instead of "similarities," "paraphrasing," and "textual appropriations" as part of King's "successful composition method." To the credit of the *Journal of American History*, when Carson submitted an article about King's plagiarisms that was replete with palaver and duplicity of this kind, the journal rejected it for disingenuousness, for a lack of forthrightness with the truth. But Carson, Bate, Engell, and McFarland are neophytes in comparison with the versatility of Keith Miller of Arizona State University, a professor of composition and the author of *Voice of Deliverance: The Language of Martin Luther King, Jr., and Its Sources* (1992).[57] Though Miller's research is indispensable for ascertaining the sources of King's most famous speeches and published works, it is riddled with absurdities, rhetorical tricks, and sophistry. For example, King's pirating was not "plagiarism" but rather "voice merging," "mining," "intertextualizations," "welding," "incorporations," "borrowings," "consulting," "absorbing," "alchemizing," "overlapping," "quarrying," "yoking," "adopting," "synthesizing," "replaying," "echoing," "resonances," and "reverberations."

Regarding Coleridge's plagiarisms, Bate and Engell eventually relied on the most time-honored excuse for pilfering, that the improprieties were unintentional and merely stemmed from careless notetaking and hasty writing. Historian Eugene Genovese, whose fine analysis of King's scholarship is found in Chapter Seven, has sympathized with this argument. As he wrote in a review of Clayborne Carson's first volume of the King *Papers* in the May 11, 1992, issue of the *New Republic*, King at times "misquoted in a manner that suggests impatience with scholarly procedures," a "sloppiness" that was "not an expression of laziness or an unwillingness to do the required work."[58] Perhaps, but how can we ever know? And since when is verbatim plagiarism a legitimate way of doing "the required work" at our universities, much less meeting the requirements of a doctoral dissertation, which by definition must be an original work of scholarship?

No one has been a more faithful defender of Clayborne Carson's editorship of the King Papers Project than Professor Genovese, and certainly no one envies the predicament in which Carson, as an editor as well as a devoted follower of King, found himself. But if scholarship — and especially publicly funded scholarship in which the scholar is serving not just Truth but the taxpayer — is to remain free of politics, platitudes, and propaganda it must rise above the unpalatable and unpleasant, and in the early days of this controversy, Carson was anything but candid about the evidence of King's plagiarisms, as Professor Genovese concedes: "As for Carson's early dissembling, I only hope that he is a Catholic, not a Protestant. For he committed a venial, not a mortal, sin and should be willing to take his chances on a short stint in purgatory."[59]

Carson's defenders — many of whom I disagree with but have included in this volume — have argued that this "early dissembling" was not an attempt to cover up the truth but merely an effort to buy time for the "scholarly process" to work. Considering the sensitive nature of this story, such dodging and pussyfooting might be understandable. But it is impossible to say how long this "dissembling" by Carson and his team might have continued without outside pressure forcing a more forthright handling of the evidence; watchdogs are never pleasant, but they do serve a purpose. But there is another problem with this argument: Carson had known about King's plagiarisms since 1987 and was still talking, as the reader will see, about "composition methods" and "textual appropriations" long after the plagiarism story had been broken and the need "to buy time" had ended, a troubling fact which Carson's defenders conveniently ignore. Simply put, Carson's duplicity gave the public that funded him and the scholarly community that trusted him little reason to expect greater candor from him in the future.

As for Professor S. Paul Schilling, who was the second reader of King's dissertation at Boston University, he pursued a path of palliation. As he stated in a letter that the university reproduces in its September 1991 report, "it should be recognized [that King] was operating on a very crowded schedule during most of the work on his dissertation," as if plagiarism is acceptable or at least excusable if one is busy and in a hurry. Schilling adds, "it should be recognized that [King's] appropriation of the language of others does not entail inaccurate interpretation of the thought of writers cited."[60] Apparently plagiarists who steal accurately deserve commendation.

Voice Merging and Civil Rights

The reader might think that, after two centuries, the conventional conceptions of literary property and literary theft would be safely and securely embedded in our culture and beyond reproach, dilution, or subversion. As Thomas Mallon wrote in 1989, "Originality — not just innocence of plagiarism but the making of something really and truly new — set itself down as a cardinal literary virtue sometime in the middle of the eighteenth century and has never since gotten up."[61] Unfortunately, in light of the King plagiarism story, we now encounter challenges from within the academy itself to subvert the traditional conceptions of authorship and originality that have persevered for two centuries as the standards for scholarship and composition.

What Thomas Mallon could not have foreseen is the rise of Keith Miller and his "voice merging" theory. Miller contends that plagiarism by certain minorities should not be condemned but rather "understood" in the context of their cultural experience. For instance, because King was black as well as a preacher, and because black preachers have traditionally viewed language as a shared commodity and "voice merged" with one another by freely swapping sermons without attribution, Miller concludes that King's plagiarisms must have derived from an inability to distinguish the classroom from the pulpit, to separate himself from this homiletic tradition, and to comprehend the standards of an alien white culture. As Miller argues in "Redefining Plagiarism" in the January 20, 1993, issue of the Chronicle of Higher Education, we must learn to "appreciate the difficulties that some [minorities] may have in negotiating the boundaries between oral and print traditions."[62] If the reader did not know better, he might conclude from Miller's articles that the "King" under discussion was a grunting savage just snatched from the jungle, instead of an intelligent and articulate man with 11 years of higher education (often at predominantly white institutions), three academic degrees, two graduate degrees, and a graduate school seminar on scholarly standards under his belt: It is exactly because King was intelligent and articulate that makes his plagiary so difficult to understand and so disheartening for King's admirers to accept.

The upshot of Miller's reasoning is that, since many minorities come from cultures rich in oral traditions, we must redefine plagiarism to accommodate these "excluded" groups. Put more bluntly, all legal claims to original thought and the interpretation of ideas must now yield in deference to multiculturalism, diversity, cultural relativism, and human rights. Like the deconstruction of Western literature and the defamation of high art, so too must the prohibition on plagiarism be ravished for the purpose of greater pluralism and cultural inclusion. As Miller states in the Chronicle of Higher Education, "the process of securing fundamental human rights such as those King championed — outweighs the right to the exclusive use of intellectual and literary property."[63] Whether we should take this logic one Marxist step forward, and abolish all private property in the name of human rights, Miller does not say.

Miller's second reason for wanting to redefine plagiarism stems specifically from King's pilfering. "We face a contradiction," he suggests in his essay. "We wish to lionize a man for his powerful language while decrying a major strategy that made his words resonate and persuade." Miller then issues a startling non sequitur: "How could such a compelling leader commit what most people define as a writer's worst sin? The contradiction should prompt us to rethink our definition of plagiarism."[64] And we should rethink drunk driving in light of Chappaquiddick; redefine adultery to account for the sins of Jimmy Swaggart; and ban all fertilizer in the wake of the Oklahoma City bombing. Miller's sophistry and skewed logic produce just such absurdities.

Miller is not alone, however, in trying to mitigate King's offense. In fact, a professor in the February 24, 1993, issue of the *Chronicle of Higher Education* not only praised Miller's essay but regretted that he "did not go far enough." For "when the purpose is to use ideas — for inspiration, practical value, clarity of purpose, good fellowship, or whatever — it can only hinder us to wonder who deserves credit for them."[65] Clayborne Carson wrote in a similar vein in the January 16, 1991, issue of the *Chronicle of Higher Education*. While "recognizing that textual appropriation was one aspect of [King's] successful composition method," says Carson, his "legitimate utilization of political, philosophical, and literary texts — particularly those expressing the nation's democratic ideals — inspired and mobilized many Americans, thereby advancing the cause of social justice."[66] Such statements, in essence, say the end justifies the means, that if one steals for the right reason — whatever "right" might mean — then the vice is excusable if not sanctionable and commendable.

Ironically, it is King's own writings that provide the best defense against the ethical and cultural relativism of King's apologists. As Eugene Genovese points out in this volume, King's own theology forbad the type of "pragmatic attitude" that Miller and company have adopted to excuse King's transgressions. In fact, King lambasted this slide of ethics into pragmatism and condemned this ends-justified-the-means mentality that led, in his words, to "lying, deceit, or violence." King, to his credit, tirelessly warned his followers to resist the temptation to use oppression and victimhood as an excuse for violence or for avoiding responsibility in their lives.

Transforming plagiarism into a virtue in light of King's pilfering is exactly Miller's aim. He accomplishes this goal through three stages in his book. He first sets the "proper" tone by opening with an epigraph from Quintilian — the first-century rhetorician whose *Institutio oratoria* is the masterwork on the subject of classical imitation.[67] The implication is clear, that both his arguments and King's plagiarisms are nothing more than a continuation of a hallowed Western tradition. His "voice merging" theory follows and prepares the reader for his bold conclusion: King's plagiarisms were perhaps his greatest gift to the country. For by "intertextualizing" stolen works into his popular speeches and essays, and by plagiarizing in particular the words and writings of liberal white preachers, King "foolproofed his discourse" and was able to "change the minds of moderate and uncommitted whites" toward solving "the nation's most horrific problem — racial injustice."[68]

There are many obvious problems with Miller's thesis. First, he argues that the plagiarisms King committed in high school, college, seminary, and graduate school stemmed from King's inability to distinguish the classroom from the pulpit but that King's plagiarisms and "voice merging" in later years were deliberately committed on behalf of the civil rights movement: this latter King, by stealing the rhetoric of white liberals, was merely "self-making" or "reinventing" himself to appeal to an entrenched and racist political establishment. In other words, according to Miller, what was an unconscious reflex derivative of a folk tradition in the 1950's had become a conscious act of political shrewdness in the 1960's. The theory is intriguing — and entirely unfounded: Miller offers no proof whatsoever for any of this. He presents nothing to prove that King either "unintentionally" plagiarized in his student days (an absurd proposition, as the reader will see) or deliberately plagiarized white sources in his later years to further the aims of the civil rights movement. Nor does he explain, regarding the latter hypothesis, why King preached before *black* audiences the same sermons cobbled together from the work of white liberal preachers.

Second, swapping sermons is certainly common among black clergy, and Martin Luther King, Jr., was indeed the product, as Richard Lischer described it in *The Preacher King* (1995), "of a preaching tradition that valued originality of effect above originality of composition."[69] But a folk art this "compositional method" may be; a hallowed *Western* tradition it has not always been. Samuel Johnson, in fact, specifically warned about the dangers of such sermon pilfering in his letter of advice to "a young clergyman in the country" in August 1780: "Take care to register, somewhere or other, the authors from whom your several discourses are borrowed; and do not imagine that you shall always remember, even what you now think it impossible to forget."[70]

Third, the idea that King plagiarized "unconsciously" is not only absurd on the face of it, as the following chapters make clear, but it is contradicted by facts and anecdotal evidence. David Garrow tells the story in *Bearing the Cross: Martin Luther King, Jr., and the Southern Christian Leadership Crisis* (1986) of an editor who turned down a book manuscript by King because it had been slapped together from huge chunks of material that King had obviously not memorized but lifted from a book he had already published; in other words, King was plagiarizing himself, something he did often in his student years. We also know that, by 1968, King's borrowings had become so prevalent that at least on one occasion they became the subject of discussion among King and his closest friends. Georgia Davis Powers, in her embarrassing tell-all autobiography of her adulterous affair with King, *I Shared the Dream: The Pride, Passion and Politics of the First Black Woman Senator From Kentucky* (1995), recounts an occasion in 1968 when King took a telephone call from his advisor Stanley Levison. After King hung up, Powers heard King muttering, "Cowardice asks, is it safe? Expediency asks, is it political? Vanity asks, is it popular? But conscience asks, is it right?" When Powers inquired whether King would use this passage from Levison in an upcoming speech, King reportedly said, "I will use it when it is appropriate." When Powers teased King and asked, "M.L., is anything we do and say original?" King smiled and replied, "Originality comes only from God."[71]

These glaring flaws in Miller's logic and argument have not, however, hindered the zest with which others have adopted his theory. The question-and-answer man of *Parade* magazine, one Walter Scott, replied in length (August 7, 1994) to a query from a reader concerned about the "rumor" of King's plagiarisms by regurgitating Miller's thesis whole hog. Instead of educating his readers about academic standards, explaining the requirements for earning the title "doctor," and delineating the different rules that govern the pulpit and the classroom, Scott, following Miller, simply whitewashed King's offense. King's pilfering was merely a misunderstanding, he explained: "King's tendency to plagiarize should be understood in the context of his background on [sic] the pulpit, where preachers borrow partly because their culture fails to define the word as a commodity and instead assumes that everyone creates language and no one owns it."[72] Considering that *Parade*'s weekly readership is in the millions, one can see how easily falsehoods, half-truths, and misinformation can spread and take root.

The "voice merging" theory has spread in particular among minority groups. "A lawyer asked me for advice in defending a Native American student charged with plagiarizing papers in law school," Miller admitted in the *Chronicle of Higher Education*. "The student came from an oral culture, and could not immediately understand or obey the rules of written English. . . . King's example thus is not an isolated case."[73] Indeed, the number of such cases should doubtless multiply: "voice merging" is a godsend to plagiarist and lawyer alike.

But what is a godsend to some is an albatross to others. For what do fair-minded scholars and good honest liberals who want to be sensitive to minority needs and who govern their lives and careers according to color-blind principles do with such theories as "voice-merging"? As one frustrated white professor from the University of Illinois explained to me in a letter in 1995, "As a person of principle, can I continue to impose tough standards on my white students after I have tolerated blatant cheating from my students of color? How do I explain to white students that they are being held accountable to higher standards by a faculty member (me) who has publicly proclaimed his insistence on color-blind rules?"

Miller's basic idea, that minorities deserve special exemption from responsibility for their literary crimes and misdemeanors, in fact lay at the root of David Leavitt's explanation of why he plagiarized the autobiography of poet Sir Stephen Spender. Leavitt admitted in an essay in the *New York Times Magazine* in 1994 that he had "used the Spender book as a source" for his novel *While England Sleeps*, especially the section in which Spender recounts a failed homosexual affair he had had in his youth; the young novelist admitted that "17 parallels" exist between his novel and Spender's book. Leavitt's "compositional method" was offensive enough, but to add insult to injury, he then embellished the plagiarized passages with lurid, fictionalized detail, which outraged Spender and sent him seeking recourse through the British courts. "I don't see why [Leavitt] should unload all his sexual fantasies onto me in my youth," complained Spender.[74]

What is significant here is Leavitt's creative defense. "Homophobia is global," he argued, and "England, a nation with no equivalent of our First Amendment, a nation that has given us Clause 28 forbidding the provision of funds for material that is seen to 'promote' homosexuality, . . . may well be on its way to becoming a nation in which writers are simply afraid to write. That, to me, is the real crime."[75] In other words, like the apologists who acknowledge King's pilfering but who excuse and even hail it as a "voice merging" strategy that was essential to our country's social and moral progress, so too does Leavitt justify his malfeasance by appropriating plagiarism as a legitimate weapon in the war for gay rights. Once again, in the words of Keith Miller, "the process of securing fundamental human rights [outweighs] the right to the exclusive use of intellectual and literary property."[76]

The Deeper Problem

The growing problem of fraud and plagiarism, and our refusal to deal with it honestly, should be reason enough to take an interest in the tale that follows, in how it unfolded and continues to develop today. But to the hundreds of individuals who have asked me in recent years, often in a prosecutorial tone, why anyone should be concerned about this story, I reply that, in a country that boasts of having the freest and most adversarial press in the world, many of our leading journals and newspapers knew about King's plagiarisms and the extent of the transgressions but suppressed the story nonetheless; that the specious propositions of Keith Miller and his followers will further undermine scholarship and composition and do greater harm than good to minority groups; that the attempt to break down the proscription on plagiarism is yet another blow to the crumbling veneer of civilized life; that what Anthony Grafton argued in *Forgers and Critics: Creativity and Duplicity in Western Scholarship* — "The exercise of criticism is a sign of health and virtue in a civilization; the prevalence of forgery is a sign of illness and vice" — holds equally true for plagiarism; and that considering the duplicity, disingenuousness, and disrespect for free debate that now are overwhelming our approach to criticism, journalism, and higher learning, we would be wise to heed Professor Grafton's remarks.[77]

But the following story is also a prime case study of racial politics today. If, as Richard Bernstein has argued, the multiculturalism/political correctness movement has "gained its moral force because of its appropriation of the mantle of the civil rights movement, its jargon and its moral fervor," then there is no better example of how the two movements have melded than the Martin Luther King, Jr., plagiarism story.[78] This story not only reflects the tensions and suspicions still palpable between the races, even after 40 years of affirmative action designed to right yesterday's wrongs, but it sets in high relief the ambivalence that still exists in dealing with the civil rights movement and its legacy, and the legacy in particular, thirty years after his death, of Martin Luther King, Jr.

Until we can tolerate dissent and frank and free discourse, forego the smear tactics designed to stifle debate, and end our obsession with gimmicks, excuses, and painless explanations for every human failing and fault, there is little hope of abating the sclerosis now crippling our critical faculties, unfettering the free spirit on which true scholarship is based, and solving the serious social and cultural problems now plaguing America and balkanizing it apart. We can opt for the status quo and take the easy way out, masking our problems with "taffeta phrases and silken terms precise," with feel-good catchwords and shibboleths like "empowerment," with speech codes, sensitivity seminars, and federally-mandated celebrations of diversity, or with novel theories of human behavior — whether "voice merging" to account for plagiarism or the "rage defense" to excuse violence — but our problems will remain and even fester from our silence and neglect. "This is the excellent foppery of the world," said Edmund to Gloucester, "that when we are sick in fortune — often the surfeits of our own behaviour — we make guilty of our disasters the sun, the moon, and stars."[79] And so we have.

The choice is ours: we and our institutions can either diagnose and deal with the "foppery" that haunts us or we can linger on collectively like a patient in deep denial. As the doctor said to the fellow stabbed in the back, "Sure, I can ease the pain and remove the knife. But I think you have a deeper problem."

CHAPTER TWO

THE STRANGE CAREER OF MARTIN LUTHER KING, JR.'S DISSERTATION

The breaking of the King plagiarism story begins not in America but in England, where a semblance of free speech and open debate still exists. On December 3, 1989, Frank Johnson, the current editor of the London *Spectator* but then a columnist for the London *Sunday Telegraph*, published a short article, under his rubric of "Mandrake," entitled "Martin Luther King, Jr. — Was He a Plagiarist?" The brief column follows:

> Researchers in his native Georgia must soon decide whether to reveal that the late Dr. Martin Luther King, murdered in 1968, was — in addition to his other human failings — a plagiarist. There is now much doubt as to whether his Ph.D. thesis was really his own work. In my view this does not detract from his greatness, no more than did the revelations about his extramarital sex life. But it is causing anguish among scholars working on his collected papers and it is bound to be said either that the accusation is false or — if true — that it should not have been made known to the world.
>
> The story has not yet been published in the United States. I heard about it from an American friend who learned it from

one of the scholars now preparing the collection of speeches, sermons, academic papers, and correspondence to be published in 12 volumes over the next 15 years. Volume one is to be published next autumn.

According to my informant, the associate editor of the project, Dr. Ralph Luker of Emory University, has discovered that Dr. King's thesis at Boston University in the early 1950's — on the theological concept known as "personalism" — lent heavily on the work, a few years before, of a white student, Jack Boozer, who went on to become a professor at Emory. Professor Boozer died not long ago.

Apparently, King mentioned Boozer's work in a footnote, but did not indicate the extent to which the thesis came from him. When I telephoned Dr. Luker at Emory and asked whether it was true that Dr. King's thesis was plagiarized, he chose his words slowly and carefully. "I have no way of responding to that," he said. "We're in the process of conducting our research, and will be able to report on that research within the next nine months."

Did Dr. King acknowledge his indebtedness to another theologian? I asked. "There is a full bibliography in the dissertation," Dr. Luker replied. Is the research team even considering the possibility of plagiarism? "It would be very foolish for us to attempt any kind of statement at this point," he replied, "because our research is not complete. When we think we know what the situation is, then we will be prepared to report it." If plagiarism is discovered, would researchers have a duty to reveal it? "Our reputations as historians are on the line," said Dr.

Luker. "I think you can draw the conclusion from that. If we thought we had a clear picture of the overall situation, and were certain of our grounds."

Dr. Clayborne Carson, of Stanford University, California, who is in overall charge of the project, said: "It's really not true" (that the thesis was plagiarized). But other remarks by him suggest that there is a problem. Asked whether the charge was completely without substance, he said: "It's hard to give a categorical answer. The answer to that question is 'no.' But it's still in the process. There is no fraud [in the dissertation]. What we're talking about is the question of whether there was adequate citation of all sources. . . . Right now, it's like calling an author before the manuscript is finished."

Despite the prodding of the *Sunday Telegraph*, the mainstream American press treated the King plagiarism story like the plague. Rumors of King's plagiarisms continued to circulate in academic circles and a few right-wing journals through mid-1990, but there remained no actual evidence of King's plagiarisms nor any acknowledgment of the story by the scholarly community or by the National Endowment of the Humanities, which funds the King Papers Project; an explosive story seemed to have died aborning. But all this changed when *Chronicles'* editor Thomas Fleming briefly referred to King's plagiarisms in his September 1990 article "Revolution and Tradition in the Humanities Curriculum": "The 'Doctor' should now be understood as strictly a courtesy title, since King, it has been recently revealed, apparently plagiarized his Boston University doctoral dissertation." This was the first mention of King's plagiarisms in the American press to garner national attention and the ire, as the reader will see, of Boston University. The following letter to *Chronicles* from B.U. President Jon Westling, then Acting B.U. President while President John Silber ran for the governorship of Massachusetts, is dated October 5, 1990. It appeared in the January 1991 issue of *Chronicles*, together with my response.

In "Revolution and Tradition in the Humanities Curriculum," Thomas Fleming repeats the false story that Dr. Martin Luther King, Jr., plagiarized his Boston University doctoral dissertation. The charge has been made several times in the last year and appears to be spreading like whooping cough among the unvaccinated. Allow me to introduce some penicillin.

Dr. King's dissertation has, in fact, been scrupulously examined and reexamined by scholars, including scholars who are thoroughly familiar with the "personalist" theological tradition to which Dr. King's dissertation was a contribution and who would stand the best chance of catching any nonattributed quotations. Not a single instance of plagiarism of any sort has been identified.

The apparent source of this defamatory rumor was an article that appeared last December in a London newspaper — an article that was refuted by its supposed primary source in a subsequent issue. To my knowledge, the reappearance of this rumor in a recent issue of *Chronicles* is the first time that any reputable journal has stumbled into this pseudo-controversy.

To set the record straight, since 1955, when Dr. King submitted his dissertation, "A Comparison of the Conceptions of God in the Thinking of Paul Tillich and Henry Nelson Wieman," not a single reader has ever found any nonattributed or misattributed quotations, misleading paraphrases, or thoughts borrowed without due scholarly reference in any of its 343 pages. If you or anyone else have evidence to the contrary, it should be presented.

My response to Mr. Westling was titled "A Doctor In Spite of Himself: The Strange Career of Martin Luther King, Jr.'s Dissertation," and it appeared in the same issue of *Chronicles* publishing Mr. Westling's letter. The issue was sent to press on October 25, 1990, two weeks before the *Wall Street Journal's* front-page story about King's plagiarisms. When the *Journal's* story appeared on November 9, *Chronicles* circulated advanced copies of my article. It was widely cited and discussed in such publications as the *Washington Post, Chicago Tribune, Chronicle of Higher Education,* and the *Journal of American History,* and it was the first article to present detailed evidence of King's plagiarisms.

As I pointed out in this essay, King received his doctorate in theology from Boston University for a 1955 dissertation entitled "A Comparison of the Conceptions of God in the Thinking of Paul Tillich and Henry Nelson Wieman." According to the rumor, King's discussion of Tillich was based on a dissertation by one Jack Stewart Boozer entitled "The Place of Reason in Paul Tillich's Concept of God," for which Boozer was awarded a Ph.D. in theology from Boston University in 1952. Boozer, who later became a professor of theology at Emory University, died in 1989. As we have seen, Dr. Clayborne Carson of Stanford University, chief editor of the King Papers Project, quickly denied that there was any validity to the rumor, telling the London *Sunday Telegraph,* "It's really not true [that the dissertation was plagiarized]." When pressed whether the charge against King was entirely without substance, he replied: "It's hard to give a categorical answer. . . .What we're talking about is the question of whether there was adequate citation of all sources." Dr. Ralph Luker of Emory University, the associate editor of the King Papers, added that a research team was considering the possibility of plagiarism. "We're in the process of conducting our research, and will be able to report on that research within the next nine months." "It would be very foolish for us to attempt any kind of statement at this point," he added, "because our research is not complete. When we think we know what the situation is, then we will be prepared to report it. . . . Our reputations as historians are on the line."

Despite the serious nature of the charge, more than nine months passed and no scholarly article appeared and no discussion of the charges occurred in our nation's press. The question was, are the plagiarism rumors true, and if true, are we dealing with a substantial case of theft or merely an instance of careless documentation? To begin with, it is worth noting that King's dissertation deals with many of the same topics found in Boozer's dissertation, and that King reaches virtually every conclusion that Boozer does concerning Tillich's conception of God — that Tillich's thought is often paradoxical if not contradictory, that Tillich sees God as "being-itself," that Tillich in the end affirms a monistic system of theology not entirely unlike Plotinus's and Hegel's, etc. Even so, it is possible to borrow a man's ideas, arguments, and evidence but paraphrase his actual language in a way that manages to stop short of plagiarism.

But, as Samuel Johnson made clear, when "there is a concurrence of more resemblances than can be imagined to have happened by chance; as where the same ideas are conjoined without any natural series or necessary coherence, or where not only the thought but the words are copied," plagiarism is surely present. This remains to date the best definition of plagiarism, and if we apply it to this case we must reach the inescapable conclusion that King plagiarized repeatedly in the course of his dissertation.

It is not merely that King's argument, language, and choice of words run parallel with Boozer's, but that whole phrases, sentences, and even paragraphs are lifted verbatim from Boozer's text. Dr. Luker of Emory is correct in pointing out that King acknowledges, on page five, that a "fine" dissertation was written on Tillich in 1952. And King does say on page seven that "the present inquiry will utilize from these valuable secondary sources any results which bear directly on the problem, and will indicate such use by appropriate footnotes." King, however, does not do this. In fact, among the dozens of sections he lifts from Boozer, he footnotes Boozer only twice, on pages 123 and 161 — and then he gets both footnotes wrong (the first quotation is found on page 193 of Boozer's text, not page 209; and the second on page 63, not page 62).

A wrong footnote here or an incorrect page number there would not warrant a discussion of plagiarism. But such slips are symptoms and signs of a much more serious offense. There is virtually no section of King's discussion of Tillich that cannot be found in Boozer's text, and often the parallels are not simply similarities but downright duplications. In other words, contrary to Dr. Carson's claim, what is involved here is by no means a mere matter of inadequate citation, as the following random examples make clear. The cumbersome footnotes King and Boozer make to Tillich's original texts have been excluded. In none of the following passages does King footnote Boozer.

On the subject of the Trinity:

King:	*Boozer:*
It is a qualitative . . . characterization of God. It is an attempt to express the richness and complexity of the divine life. . . . It is the abysmal character of God, the element of power which is the basis of the Godhead, "which makes God God." (pp. 152-153)	. . . it is a qualitative characterization of God. It is an effort to express the richness of the divine life. . . . It is the abysmal character of God, the element of power, which is the basis of the Godhead, "which makes God God." (p. 214)

On dualism:

King:	*Boozer:*
[Dualism] is aware of the two poles of reality, but dualism conceives these in a static complementary relationship. Tillich maintains that these poles are related in dynamic interaction, that one pole never exists out of relation to the other pole. Herein is one of Tillich's basic criticisms of Hegel. Hegel, according to Tillich, transcends the tension of existential involvement in the concept of a synthesis. (p. 25)	Dualism is aware of the two poles of reality, but dualism conceives these in a static complementary relationship. Tillich maintains that they are related in a dynamic interaction, that one pole never exists out of relation to the other pole. One feels here again that . . . Tillich criticizes Hegel. For, according to Tillich, Hegel transcends the tension of existential involvement in the concept of a synthesis. (p. 268)

On God's manifestation in history:

King:

In a real sense, then,
God manifests himself
in history. This
manifestation is never
complete because God as
abyss is inexhaustible. But
God as logos is manifest
in history and is in real
interdependence with
man.
(p. 27)

Boozer:

In a real sense, then . . .
God manifests himself
in history. This
manifestation is never
complete because God as
abyss is inexhaustible. But
God as logos is manifest
in history and is in real
interdependence with
man and man's logos.
(p. 270)

On correlation:

King:	*Boozer:*
Correlation means correspondence of data in the sense of a correspondence between religious symbols and that which is symbolized by them. It is upon the assumption of this correspondence that all utterances about God's nature are made. This correspondence is actual in the logos nature of God and the logos nature of man. (p. 21)	Correlation means correspondence of data in the sense of a correspondence between religious symbols and that which is symbolized by them. It is upon the assumption of this correspondence that all utterances about God's nature are made. This correspondence is actual in the logos-nature of God and the logos-nature of man. (p. 265)

On symbol and sign:

King:	*Boozer:*
A symbol possesses a necessary character. It cannot be exchanged. A sign, on the contrary, is impotent and can be exchanged at will. A religious symbol is not the creation of a subjective desire or work. If the symbol loses its ontological grounding, it declines and becomes a mere "thing," a sign impotent in itself. "Genuine symbols are not interchangeable at all and real symbols provide no objective knowledge, but yet a true awareness." The criterion of a symbol is that through it the unconditioned is clearly grasped in its unconditionedness. Correlation as the correspondence of data	A symbol possesses a necessary character. It cannot be exchanged. On the other hand a sign is impotent in itself and can be exchanged at will. . . . The religious symbol is not the creation of a subjective desire or work. If the symbol loses its ontological grounding, it declines and becomes a mere "thing," a sign impotent in itself. "Genuine symbols are not interchangeable at all and real symbols provide no objective knowledge, but yet a true awareness." The criterion of a symbol is that through it the unconditioned is clearly grasped in its unconditionedness. . . . (p. 125) Correlation as the correspondence of data

means in this particular
case that there is
correspondence between
religious symbols and that
reality which these
symbolize. Once a true
religious symbol is
discovered one can be
sure that here is an
implicit indication of
the nature of God.
(pp. 22-24)

means in this particular
case that there is
correspondence between
religious symbols and that
reality which these
symbolize. Once a true
religious symbol has been
discovered one can be
sure that here is an
implicit indication of
the nature of God.
(p. 267)

This last example is particularly revealing, because it shows not only the extent of King's plagiary but his habit of pasting together disparate sections of Boozer's text, in this case sections that are more than 100 pages apart. This conjoining of different sections of Boozer's dissertation could not have been done without great circumspection and forethought; it gives the lie to the notion that King somehow plagiarized unintentionally.

The citations of such parallels could go on for many pages. King on freedom, page 312, is taken from pages 62 and 63 of Boozer. King on the "real interdependence of things and events," pages 25 and 26, is taken from page 269 of Boozer. King on the omnipresence of God, page 292, is taken from page 197 of Boozer. King on naturalism, or "humanism," page 18, is taken from pages 262 and 263 of Boozer. Et cetera.

As any devotee of detective stories well knows, it is the slight slips and blunders that most often carry the gravest consequence for the perpetrator of the crime. It is the dropped cuff link or forgotten matchbook that often reveals the perpetrator's identity and seals his fate, and King and his dissertation are no exceptions. King's forgotten matchbook and dropped cuff link are a comma and a typo.

Amid a discussion of Tillich's conception of "creation," we find the following parallel:

King:	Boozer:
But Tillich does not mean by creation an event which took place "once upon a time." Creation does not refer to an event, it rather indicates a condition, a relationship between God and the world. "It is the correlate to the analysis of man's <u>finitude, it</u> answers the question implied in man's finitude and infinitude [sic] generally." Man asks a question which, in existence, he cannot answer. But the . . . (p. 125)	But Tillich does not mean by creation an event which took place "once upon a time." Creation does not describe an event, it rather indicates a condition, a relationship between God and the world. "It is the correlate to the analysis of man's <u>finitude, it</u> answers the question implied in man's finitude and in finitude generally." Man asks a question which, in existence, he cannot answer. But the . . . (pp. 45-46)

King has not only lifted this entire passage from Boozer's text (in fact, the verbatim plagiarism continues well beyond the last sentence cited above) but has even copied an error in punctuation. The grammatically incorrect comma between the two underlined words in both paragraphs does not appear in Tillich's text, which is correctly punctuated with a period. Boozer, in quoting these lines from page 252 of volume one of Tillich's *Systematic Theology*, mistakenly copied the period as a comma, and King simply copied Boozer's mistake.

More problems arise in the pages concluding King's section on Tillich. On page 159, King says he is now coming to the question that has been "cropping up throughout our discussion of Tillich's God-concept, viz., the question of whether Tillich holds to an absolute quantitative monism." The reader can feel the buildup to King's exposition of his thesis, one of the pivotal points to which his dissertation — his original contribution to scholarship on which his title of "doctor" would forever rest — has been leading. Once again, this just happens to be one of the critical questions to which Boozer also builds. As Boozer states on page 60, "We come now to a crucial issue for an understanding of Tillich. Is man a part of God in an absolute quantitative monism?" Virtually every line of King's concluding remarks on pages 159 and 160 can be found on pages 60 through 63 of Boozer's dissertation:

King:	*Boozer:*
Perhaps Tillich's most explicit statement of monism is his contention that "man's love of God is the love with which God loves himself. . . . The divine life is the divine self-love." . . . Passages such as these cited indicate an absolute monism. . . . Tillich affirms that there would be no history unless man were to some degree free; that is, to some extent, independent from God. . . . He [man] is to some extent "outside" the divine life. This means that he stands "in actualized freedom, in an existence which is no longer united with essence." (p. 160)	But perhaps the most convincing statement of monism is in terms of love, that "man's love of God is the love with which God loves himself. . . . The divine life is the divine self-love." . . . Passages such as these certainly indicate an absolute monism. . . . There would be no history unless man were to some degree free; that is, to some degree independent from God. . . . He [man] is to some extent "outside" the divine life. "To be outside the divine life means to stand in actualized freedom, in an existence which is no longer united with essence." (pp. 62-63)

King embarrassingly even claims Boozer's conclusions as his own. Boozer, page 61: "The similarity of Tillich's theology with Hegel's philosophy of spirit and Plotinus' philosophy of the One inclines one to interpret Tillich as an absolute monist." King, pages 159-160: "The similarity of Tillich's view at this point to Hegel's philosophy of spirit and Plotinus' philosophy of the One inclines one to interpret Tillich as an absolute monist."

It is amid these concluding remarks that King commits another error. King quotes the following from Tillich on page 159 of his thesis: "God is infinite because he has the finite within himself united with his infinity." Boozer uses this same quotation on page 61 of his thesis. Boozer, however, mistakenly credits it to page 282 of volume one of Tillich's *Systematic Theology*, whereas the correct page number is 252. King again copies Boozer's mistake and also types page 282 for his footnote. Boozer's next line in this paragraph is another quotation from page 252 of Tillich's text — "The divine life is creative, actualizing itself in inexhaustible abundance." King follows with the same quotation. This time, however, Boozer correctly cites page 252 in his footnote. King, still following Boozer's previous mistake, continues incorrectly to cite page 282.

No further evidence is needed to conclude that King plagiarized his doctoral dissertation. But many questions remain, such as how Professor L. Harold DeWolf, the first reader of both Boozer's and King's dissertations, could have overlooked — intentionally or unintentionally — the similarities between the two theses. And what are we to make of the disingenuous statements made by the editors of the King Papers, whose reputations — by their own admission — were on the line? The idea that they needed nine months to review the evidence before issuing a statement is absurd. A few hours with each text is all that was necessary.

The King plagiarism story was suppressed for one simple reason: fear — fear of the massive retaliation that would be visited upon anyone who attempted to set the historical record straight, not just on King and his dissertation but on any historical incident or person on which the powers that be have declared an official position. Perhaps I and *Chronicles* would have been wiser had we ignored this entire matter. But evidence of a cover-up made up our minds. We learned, for example, that high-level administrators at several major universities had attempted to suppress this story and that at least one scholar had been bullied into silence. We also wondered why the National Endowment for the Humanities, which funds the King Papers Project and was well aware of the charge of plagiarism, had yet to take any action.

But other academic issues were also at stake. As Stephen Nissenbaum, one of the most noted victims of plagiarism in recent years, remarked in the *Chronicle of Higher Education* (March 28, 1990): "To be willing to pass judgment is to protect everybody — not only those who are victimized by plagiarism, but also those who are falsely accused of it."

Then there was the reproof administered by the "ad interim" president of Boston University. Mr. Westling insisted that scholars had "scrupulously examined and reexamined" King's dissertation without being able to identify "a single instance of plagiarism" — no "misattributed quotations," no "misleading paraphrases," and no "thoughts borrowed without due scholarly reference." He concluded his letter with this challenge: "If you or anyone else have evidence to the contrary, it should be presented." We issued a similar challenge, at the close of my essay, to Mr. Westling, the editors of the King Papers, and all other interested scholars: if you have any genuine evidence that might exonerate King, it should be presented.

Two final comments. Gerald McKnight argues in *The Last Crusade: Martin Luther King, Jr., the FBI, and the Poor People's Campaign* (1998) that King's plagiary was not only the "most deep-dyed of academic transgressions," but it actually put the entire "black freedom struggle" at risk. For if J. Edgar Hoover had examined King's writings and discovered the plagiary, there is no doubt that he would have used this information to destroy King's career early on in the civil rights movement. McKnight assumes that no one else could have successfully led the "black freedom struggle," perhaps a questionable assumption. But his point is well taken nonetheless: that "the [FBI] missed this singular window of opportunity to destroy King diminishes the carefully cultivated image of the Hoover-era FBI . . . as omnipotent and omniscient."

Second, in their introduction to *We Shall Overcome: Martin Luther King, Jr., and the Black Freedom Struggle* (1993), editors Peter Albert and Ronald Hoffman argue that King's legend has actually impeded the progress of civil rights in the United States. For by lionizing the man, the movement has lost sight of the actual grassroots work on which success depends. This, of course, is nothing different from what Martin Luther King, Jr.'s best friend, the late Reverend Ralph Abernathy, had been saying all along: that the best thing King's supporters could do for themselves, for the movement, and for King is to celebrate the leader's virtues, his talents, his dreams, but not to make him into something he never was and something no man could ever be.

CHAPTER THREE

THE ANATOMY OF A SCOOP

The news blackout on the King plagiarism story ended here in America when the *Wall Street Journal* ran an article by Peter Waldman entitled "To Their Dismay, King Scholars Find a Troubling Pattern — Civil Rights Leader Was Lax in Attributing Some Parts of His Academic Papers." The story appeared on November 9, 1990, two weeks after *Chronicles* had gone to press with my story on King's plagiarized dissertation. As Waldman explained, the students and scholars who discovered King's plagiary were shocked, deeply troubled, and angered by their findings. What Waldman did not discuss are the many newsmen, editors, publishers, and scholars who had long known about King's plagiary but refused to report the story. The following, as a consequence, appeared as a shocking page-one scoop.

    Six years before his death, the Reverend Martin Luther King, Jr., donated a large collection of his papers to Boston University. But the rest of his writings remained in his private study in Atlanta and scattered in church basements and file cabinets from coast to coast. In 1984, Mr. King's widow, Coretta Scott King, founded the Martin Luther King, Jr., Papers Project to collect the papers and produce a multivolume collection. And she chose Clayborne Carson, a Stanford University historian, to lead the project.

Now, Mr. Carson, and his fellow researchers at Stanford, admirers of Mr. King, have found something they wish they had never discovered. They say that during his seven years of graduate school, Mr. King borrowed words and ideas extensively from other sources for his doctoral dissertation and other scholarly writings without giving proper citations. "Several of King's academic papers, as well as his dissertation, contain numerous appropriated passages that can be defined as plagiarism," says Mr. Carson, senior editor and director of the project.

For instance, in parts of Mr. King's doctoral dissertation at Boston University, he used the same general structure, many of the same words and the same section titles as another doctoral dissertation written a few years earlier at the university. Though Mr. King paid tribute to his predecessor's work on the fifth page of his dissertation and cited it again in his bibliography, he footnoted the heavily borrowed text just twice in the course of the 343-page dissertation.

The project's discoveries have stirred debate, anguish, and soul-searching among scholars who have worked on the project. They have kept the findings secret for nearly three years. Several student-researchers wondered why the information should be probed. Some resigned. One summer intern broke down in tears when she found out. Megan Maxwell, who joined the project as a Stanford undergraduate and became assistant archivist after graduation, says her initial reaction was anger, "a combination of 'Why didn't anyone catch him?' and 'Why didn't he know better?'" Associate Editor Ralph Luker, a follower of Mr. King who was jailed during a civil rights protest, says he suffered "deep anxieties" over it and "many hours of lost sleep."

Seeing the extent of Mr. King's borrowings "had a tremendously shaking, emotional impact on me," says David Garrow, a member of the project's advisory board and author of *Bearing the Cross*, a Pulitzer Prize-winning biography of Mr. King. "To me, 98 percent of what makes it most interesting is: Why did he do it? Was he so insecure that he thought this was the only way to get by? It's disconcerting, because it is fundamentally, phenomenally out of character with my entire sense of the man."

Mr. King's school papers comprise his most obscure and insignificant writings. They tended to explore esoteric themes within theology and had little to do with his ability to electrify the nation as a Baptist preacher and civil rights leader with his eloquent pleas for racial justice. In 1964, he was awarded the Nobel Peace Prize, and in 1984 Congress declared his birthday a federal holiday.

The discovery is part of a revisionist picture of Mr. King that has been emerging from recent books and academic papers. Those point up some of his human flaws and portray him as less of a myth and more of a man, as more of a brilliant leader than a ground-breaking thinker. Perhaps the most controversial was Ralph Abernathy's recent autobiography, which includes allegations that Mr. King spent time with a woman friend the last night of his life.

A book due out next spring will examine the origins of many of Mr. King's speeches, sermons, and essays. Author Keith Miller, a professor of rhetoric and composition at Arizona State

University, won't comment on his research. But in two academic articles published in 1986 and last January, Mr. Miller shows how passages in Mr. King's books *Strength to Love* and *Stride Toward Freedom* and in his famous essay "Letter From Birmingham City Jail" echoed parts of sermons and books by several ministers and writers, particularly Harry Emerson Fosdick, who was at Riverside Church in New York, and Harris Wofford, author of a book on nonviolence and now Pennsylvania's labor secretary. For example, Mr. Miller points out, Mr. King echoed Mr. Fosdick nearly word-for-word when he wrote: "Any religion that professes to be concerned about the souls of men and is not concerned about the slums that damn them . . . is a spiritually moribund religion."

Mr. Miller believes Mr. King's technique stemmed from the oral traditions of the black church. There, words weren't regarded as private property but as a shared resource for the community. He and others believe Mr. King excelled at "voice merging," as scholars call it, blending other people's words with his own.

From 1948 to 1955, Mr. King received high marks as a divinity student at Crozer Theological Seminary in Pennsylvania, where he graduated at the top of his class, and then as a doctoral candidate at Boston University. The questions about his academic work surfaced in late 1987, nearly 20 years after his death. A Stanford graduate student working for the King Papers Project found that, in some parts of Mr. King's dissertation, he lifted passages nearly word-for-word from other texts without using any quotation marks or footnotes. In other places in his dissertation Mr. King used quotation marks and footnotes to mark part of a passage, but after the quotation marks ended, the borrowed text continued. Another project researcher discovered the similarities to the earlier dissertation.

After those issues surfaced, Mr. Carson asked his staff to check the sources of nearly all of Mr. King's academic work. A pattern emerged. Most of Mr. King's papers had many original thoughts. But throughout the seven years of graduate school, Mr. King's essays, particularly in his major field of graduate study, systematic theology, often borrowed without citing them in accordance with academic rules.

For the 46-year-old Mr. Carson, the discovery of Mr. King's questionable citation practices became an unwelcome obsession. Mr. Carson attended his first civil rights demonstration as a college freshman in 1963 — the legendary March on Washington, where he heard Mr. King's "I Have a Dream" speech — and later was jailed for participating in a protest. As editor of the King Papers, however, Mr. Carson has been determined "to keep a balance between the tendency to idealize and the tendency to debunk," he says. "My job is to explain, not to defend and not to attack."

The role has been an exasperating one. After the citation problems emerged, three project editors and a half-dozen student-researchers spent nearly two years annotating all of Mr. King's 150 or so academic papers. The long digression not only kept editors and students from doing more interesting research, but it threw the project's first volume, originally due out this January, 16 months behind schedule. The delay strained the

finances of the project, funded mostly by the National Endowment for the Humanities and Stanford.

Mr. Carson tries not to be judgmental about the discoveries.
He asked staff members to refrain from using the word "plagiarism" around the office, giving rise among the scholars to the
euphemism "the p-word." But that doesn't prevent Mr. Carson
and his fellow researchers from trying to figure out the central
question: Why?

Mr. King's academic papers demonstrated that he had a
working knowledge of the use of footnotes, bibliographies, and
other conventions. Records show that he took a thesis-writing
class at Boston University in which the teacher lectured on
proper methods of citation. Somewhere, in most of Mr. King's
scholarly essays, he cited the sources from which he borrowed
material, though those citations rarely indicated the extent of
his appropriations.

It is doubtful that Mr. King intended to slip anything past
his dissertation adviser, L. Harold DeWolf. Three years before
Mr. King completed his dissertation, Mr. DeWolf had been the
doctoral adviser for a student named Jack Boozer, author of the
dissertation that Mr. King so heavily relied on in parts of his
own. Mr. DeWolf's signature appeared on the approval pages
of both dissertations. (Mr. Boozer died in 1989. His wife, Ruth,
says he learned about the project's findings shortly before his
death. "He told me he'd be so honored and so glad if there
were anything that Martin Luther King could have used from
his work," she says.) Mr. Carson guesses that Mr. King didn't
think he was doing anything wrong. "The best evidence for

that," he says, "is that he saved his papers and donated them to an archive — at B.U. of all places."

Mr. King wrote much of his dissertation in 1954, after becoming pastor of Dexter Avenue Baptist Church in Montgomery, Alabama. He worked on the manuscript early in the morning and late at night, according to biographical accounts, while instituting a number of church programs and preaching at churches and colleges across the South. "It was possible that the press of his work caused him to be careless," suggests Cornish Rogers, a friend and classmate of Mr. King's at Boston University and now a professor at the School of Theology at Claremont, California.

Several researchers at the project have focused much of their disappointment on Mr. King's professors, who they say must have recognized the problems but didn't act. "Their assumption was they were training someone to go teach in a predominantly black college in the South," says Penny Russell, who worked for five years as administrator and associate editor of the King Papers Project. "Were they setting up different standards?"

Mr. DeWolf, Mr. King's doctoral adviser, has died. S. Paul Schilling, the so-called second reader of Mr. King's dissertation at Boston University, has reviewed the project's findings. He says that Mr. King's dissertation was among the first he ever evaluated and that "I was not sufficiently perceptive in regard to plagiarism." Mr. Schilling did warn Mr. King in an early draft of the dissertation that he had "almost exactly quoted" another writer without using quotation marks, but Mr. King didn't make the suggested revisions. Mr. Schilling vehemently denies that he or Mr. DeWolf had any double standards.

All of this presented difficult issues to the project. Among them: How should the project reveal its findings? And should the project use footnotes in the volumes to note each borrowed passage? Not only would that dramatically increase the length of the books, but Mr. Carson worried about the visual impact of page after page of footnotes occupying as much or more space as Mr. King's own writing.

The issues were discussed in October 1989 at a meeting in Atlanta of the King Papers Project's advisory board. Mrs. King presided. She opened the meeting with a prayer and thanked the dozen or so scholars for their attendance. For the rest of the all-day meeting, Mrs. King said almost nothing, registering little emotion on her face, according to people in attendance. Through a spokesman, she deferred inquiries for this article to Mr. Carson.

After several hours of sometimes emotional discussion, the advisory board agreed that Mr. Carson should do two things: publish the academic papers with complete footnotes, regardless of the visual effect, and write a separate scholarly article, outlining and interpreting the citation problems. In June, Mr. Carson submitted a paper on Mr. King's use of citations to the *Journal of American History*. It was rejected. Neither Mr. Carson nor the journal will discuss why. But project staff members say the journal criticized Mr. Carson's unwillingness to take a firm stand on the question of plagiarism. Mr. Carson is revising the piece for resubmission. (Last week, when he learned the *Wall Street Journal* was preparing this article, he agreed to be interviewed.) If accepted, his article will probably appear in the

Journal of American History's June issue. Staff members say he is addressing the question of plagiarism more directly and may include a chart showing the approximate percentages in the dissertation of Mr. King's own words and the words of others. For now, Mr. Carson will say only that a "substantial" amount was borrowed.

Mr. Carson does not have an easy task. Says Mr. Luker, the associate editor, who is based at Emory University: "Clayborne has to achieve a position that is politically viable in the black community, politically respectable and acceptable in the academic community, and maintain a friendly relationship with Mrs. King."

Why did it take so long for American journalists to report this sensational story to the public? Charles Babington's article "Embargoed" in the January 28, 1991, issue of the *New Republic* answered this question and exposed the many publishers and editors who had long known about King's plagiarisms but refused to cover the story:

On November 9, 1990, the *Wall Street Journal* published what was widely seen as a solid, page-one scoop: Martin Luther King, Jr., had plagiarized parts of his doctoral dissertation. The next day the rest of the press followed with front-page stories, crediting the *Journal* for the news. What they didn't reveal was that many of them had had the story themselves — a story that had been widely rumored, and easily available, for a year — and not printed it. The *Washington Post*, the *New York Times*, the *Atlanta Journal/Constitution*, and the *New Republic* had all failed to run articles even though at least one editor at each journal knew of the King story last spring, and three right-wing journals had already published it.

The story begins on December 3, 1989 — 11 months before the *Wall Street Journal's* coup. The *Sunday Telegraph* of London carried an article headlined: "Martin Luther King, Jr. — Was He a Plagiarist?" The column, by Frank Johnson under the pen name Mandrake, said, "Researchers in his native Georgia must soon decide whether to reveal that the late Dr. King . . . was — in addition to his other human failings — a plagiarist." The column even identified the smoking gun — the dissertation of fellow Boston University student Jack Boozer, from whom King lifted large passages verbatim. Mandrake quoted Ralph Luker of Atlanta, top assistant to Clayborne Carson. Luker virtually confirmed the allegations with his painstaking efforts to sidestep all questions about plagiarism. As a final goad, Mandrake wrote, "The story has not yet been published in the United States." Johnson says he got the King plagiarism story from a British professor who had visited the United States, and that he's not surprised the U.S. press ignored his article. "American reporters' powers of perception tend to fail them on questions of race, gender, gays," he told me.

Articles in the *Sunday Telegraph* (circulation 585,000) are available through Nexis, the computer database service used by many U.S. news organizations and businesses. Any reporter who heard the talk of King's plagiarism in early 1990 could have had Mandrake's road map in minutes by asking Nexis for articles containing the words "Martin Luther King" and "plagiarism." From there, a visit to Boston University's library —

which contains both Boozer's and King's dissertations — would have provided the information for the story.

On January 22, 1990, *The Spotlight*, the Liberty Lobby's organ, which claims a circulation of 100,000, carried a front-page story: "King Stole PhD Thesis, According to Evidence." The article, next to an item on "QUEER legislation" and an ad for a $5 cassette on "Alcohol, the Devil's A Bomb," rehashed the Mandrake column. It also included its own interview with Luker, who again refused to confirm or deny the plagiarism charge.

From March 1 to 3 about fifty members of the Southern Intellectual History Circle met in Chapel Hill, North Carolina. "It was very clear that the story [of King's plagiarism] was in the academic cocktail-party gossip network by then," says Luker, who attended. One conferee was University of North Carolina sociologist John Shelton Reed, and he soon began drafting his monthly column for *Chronicles*, the magazine of The Rockford Institute in Illinois. He cited the *Telegraph* story, and the gossip in American academia. So widespread is the talk, he continued, "I presume that by the time this letter sees print I won't be telling you anything you don't know."

But Reed balked at publishing. He was surprised the U.S. press still had not written about the plagiarism as his June publication date neared, and says he didn't care to see headlines saying, "Reed alleges King plagiarism." In his proposed column Reed called on B.U. to replace King's Ph.D. with an honorary doctorate. As a courtesy, he mailed a copy to the university's interim president, Jon Westling. Westling responded with "a stern letter" insisting that the allegations were totally false, Reed says. At the last minute Reed withdrew his column. (As late as October Westling wrote *Chronicles* saying King's "dissertation has, in fact, been scrupulously examined and reexamined by scholars. . . . Not a single instance of plagiarism of any sort has been identified.")

In September, peeved by his columnist's fickleness, *Chronicles* editor Thomas Fleming wrote an article saying, "King, it has been recently revealed, apparently plagiarized his Boston University doctoral dissertation." Meanwhile, *Chronicles* assistant editor Theodore Pappas obtained copies of the King and Boozer dissertations, located extensive examples of King's filching, and laid them out in an article. It ran in January's issue, which, he says, "we had already put together" when the *Wall Street Journal* article appeared.

By mid-1990, Clayborne Carson realized that talk of the plagiarism — which he had known about since late 1987 — was seeping out. He held a handful of reporters at bay by misleading them about the extent of the problem. Scholars and government officials, meanwhile, agreed to remain silent.

In early 1990, Carson's team told its main underwriter, the National Endowment for the Humanities, of the plagiarism. (Lynne Cheney and fellow officials were not obligated to divulge the information, NEH spokesmen say. And they didn't.) The previous October Carson had described his discoveries to Mrs. King and the project's board of directors. They agreed he should include the findings in a scholarly article for the quarterly *Journal of American History*, to be published in December

1990. The *Journal*, however, rejected his first draft in a dispute over how to address the plagiarism matter. Carson and his colleagues began revising the piece for a mid-1991 issue. Meanwhile, word of the plagiarism was leaking from Atlanta-based scholars and former students who had worked with the King Papers team at Emory University. That group, unlike Carson's Stanford-based contingent, had the Boozer dissertation, which is why press attention came to focus on the borrowing from Boozer. In fact, Carson says, King's greatest source of plagiarized material came from the theologian Paul Tillich.

The first U.S. reporter to approach Carson with questions about plagiarism was the *Washington Post*'s Dan Balz. Balz says he interviewed Carson last spring and received "a less alarmist view of what they had" about the plagiarism. Balz, unaware of the Mandrake column, knew nothing of Boozer. He says the *Post* did a database search, but asked for information about the King Papers Project rather than "King" and "plagiarism." Balz says Carson told him, "Once we've got all the evidence assembled, you can come out and look at it and draw your own conclusions." Balz agreed, after obtaining what he thought was Carson's promise to alert him if other reporters came snooping around. Through the summer and early fall, Carson kept telling Balz that his researchers needed more time. When I asked Carson if he had led Balz to believe there was less to the plagiarism story than there really was, he replied: "Definitely. I don't apologize for the fact I tried to play it down. . . . I wasn't about to break the story to someone who just asked" about King's plagiarism in general terms.

By autumn Carson got a call from Peter Waldman, the Atlanta-based *Wall Street Journal* reporter who eventually got the scoop. At first Carson did his usual stonewalling. "I told him the same thing — no big deal, don't call us, we'll call you," Carson says. But a few weeks later Waldman called him back to tell him he had the Boozer dissertation. According to Carson, Waldman said, "We'll go to press with or without you." Carson cooperated.

What had happened at the *Post?* Despite the paper's troubled relations with black readers, Balz and deputy managing editor Robert Kaiser say the paper didn't deliberately drag its feet on the King story. Kaiser says the paper exercised normal caution "because of the problem of besmirching people's reputations on the basis of hearsay." The *Post's* ombudsman, Richard Harwood, agrees, but adds: "I suspect that we pursue more rapidly and vigorously things about some people than we do about other people."

The *Atlanta Journal/Constitution* has no one to blame but itself. Frances Schwartzkopff, a rookie suburban reporter, picked up the plagiarism rumor last spring from the same source that Waldman did — a former Emory student who had worked on the King editing project. Hesitating at first out of concern for the source, she says, "I told my editors after a month or so." That triggered a debate about who should handle the story, how to pursue it, etc. It's unclear exactly what happened, but the reporter finally assigned to the story knew nothing of Schwartzkopff's information (including the Boozer connection) and started reporting from scratch.

The *New York Times* was even more hapless. An editor for the paper's book review section learned of King's plagiarisms from a prominent historian, who swore the editor to secrecy in early 1990. Rebecca Sinkler, editor of the *New York Times Book Review*, says the paper has a strict policy of telling the news staff about newsworthy tips. "I certainly never heard diddly about this," she says. When I asked Anthony DePalma, the *Times* reporter who followed up the *Wall Street Journal*'s scoop, about reports that a book review sub-editor had sat on the story, he said he'd heard the same story, and tried to learn the editor's identity, to no avail.

At the *New Republic*, literary editor Leon Wieseltier learned of the King plagiarism last spring from Eugene Genovese, a historian now living in Atlanta. "I thought it was a story that was going to stir people, and could easily be put to all sorts of unpleasant purposes," Wieseltier says. So the magazine's editors "decided early on — I think correctly, since this was a story about ideas and texts — that it would require a certain amount of scholarly skill" from the writer. The magazine approached several historians, all of whom took some time to consider, and decline, the assignment. But sentimentality and "correct politics" inhibited the editors from vigorously pursuing the story. In retrospect, says Martin Peretz, the *New Republic*'s editor in chief, the magazine reacted too gingerly because of the story's racial overtones. "Everybody suddenly got palsied," he says.

Carson, who was less than forthcoming until the *Wall Street Journal* got the goods, can take some pride in his buying of time before the plagiarism story broke. "Looking back," he says, "it might have been naive to think it would wait for the scholarly process to work. But it almost worked."

What certainly did work was the attempt to squash any debate on the King plagiarism story. Aiding those wanting to circumscribe discussion of this story was the national outrage then raging over Arizona's failure to enact a state-wide paid holiday in honor of King. William Murchison of the *Dallas Morning News* was the only nationally syndicated journalist to pick up on this and to see the tie between these three related matters: the King plagiarism story, the Arizona holiday controversy, and the national pressure that was exerted to prevent a frank and free discussion of these issues. His December 5, 1990, column follows:

> Anybody else out there tired of letting Arizona off lightly? The rubber hose isn't working. We cancel sports events and conventions scheduled in Arizona, and there is still no Martin Luther King holiday.
>
> My fellow vigilantes, why don't we really show 'em? Why not a nuclear strike on Arizona? Let's get it over with. No state that won't honor Dr. King with a *paid* day off deserves to live. Isn't that, after all, what we're supposed to conclude from the relentless boom-boom of anti-Arizona propaganda? You'd think, to hear all the yelps for vengeance, that the voters of Arizona had offered to fund a retirement community for SS camp guards.
>
> In fact, all the voters have done is assert their prerogative as voters — the same prerogative all Americans enjoy. They expressed an opinion. The opinion goes down poorly with the pure-hearted and righteous, who consider Arizona a reprobate

state, deserving of hell fire and damnation. The specific of-fense was overturning a Martin Luther King holiday that had been voted by the legislature. Is this any of our business — we Texans, New Yorkers, Floridians, Coloradans? We don't live in Arizona, do we? Don't pay taxes there, do we? What's it to us if Arizona honors Martin Luther King or Madonna? How does it touch our lives one way or the other?

Ah, but that's just in theory. The way this thing plays out in practice is that Arizona has affronted the civilized world. Seems that we were all waiting (whether we knew it or not) for Arizona's electorate to affirm the King holiday, and they let *us* down.

The bashing and kicking has proceeded apace. National Football League (NFL) Commissioner Paul Tagliabue wants to yank the 1993 Super Bowl out of Phoenix (which, ironically, observes Martin Luther King day at the local level). The Uni-versity of Virginia Cavaliers decline cavalierly to play in the Sunkist Fiesta Bowl at Tempe — assuming the game isn't moved out of state. The 1994 National Basketball Association (NBA) All-Star's game in Phoenix is called off. And the National League of Cities has pulled its December 1991 convention out of Phoenix.

What is going on here? Has the late Dr. King attained so exalted a position in the celestial choir that opposition to a paid King holiday — now observed in all but three states — is to be equated with blasphemy? How absurd! How — to use an old-fashioned, but still-meaningful, word — un-American! Dr. King, the man, was, after all, a *man*, with strengths and weak-nesses. Ralph David Abernathy has written of his friend's moral failings. Lately it has been demonstrated that Mr. King got to be "Dr." King in part through plagiarism. Theodore Pappas, who made a line-by-line comparison of King's Ph.D. dissertation with that of one Jack Boozer, writes in the January issue of *Chronicles* that "whole phrases, sentences, and even paragraphs are lifted verbatim from Boozer's test. . . . There is virtually no section of King's discussion of [Paul] Tillich that cannot be found in Boozer's text, and often the parallels are not simply similarities but downright duplications."

Have Arizona's voters no moral right to wrestle with such considerations? Indeed, is this not a profounder matter than any relating to King's character — the right to judge, the right to say yes, or to say no? The National League of Cities and the NBA would strip Arizona of that intensely American right. Arizona has the right to agree with the league and the NBA. Oh, yes. But to disagree, even in good conscience; to express a contrary opinion: No, no, a thousand times no!

It is hard to see that Dr. King, who died for the right to choose, would be beguiled by the movement to browbeat, in his name, the right to free expression of opinion. It is at least possible he would be appalled, as all Americans, whatever their political convictions, should be appalled.

It's none of our business what Arizona does. Let Arizona alone. If the rest of us worked as hard cleaning up our own backyards as we're working to clean up Arizona, we'd all be better off. Holy Writ offers the Arizona-bashers a splendid but so-far-unheeded piece of advice: "Before you remove the splinter from your brother's eye, make sure you've pried the beam from your own eye."

Of course, the Arizona-bashers had no intention of letting up. And they eventually won, for Arizonans were indeed punished for their politically incorrect vote. Though Phoenix celebrated a city-wide day in honor of King, this was deemed insufficient gratitude by the Torquemada of professional football, Paul Tagliabue, who announced at the NFL owners' auto-da-fé in March 1991 that the 1993 Super Bowl would be moved from Phoenix to either San Diego or Pasadena. Tagliabue hinted that if Arizonans would recant their heathen ways — i.e., the exercising of their democratic rights — by voting in a state-wide *paid* holiday for King, the NFL might grace the Valley of the Sun with a Super Bowl at a later date.

To anyone who believes voting costs nothing in America — think again.

CHAPTER FOUR

PLAGIARISM FOR PROGRESS

The story of Martin Luther King, Jr.'s plagiarism elicited a number of responses, most of them disingenuous. For example, in a letter to the editor published in the April 1991 issue of *Chronicles*, the former dean of Boston University's School of Theology, one Walter Muelder, tried to exculpate B.U.'s Jon Westling but only succeeded in making matters worse. Mr. Muelder's letter did confirm one fact: from beginning to end, from the December 1989 interview with the London *Sunday Telegraph* to the present, King Papers editor Clayborne Carson has consistently misrepresented the facts and distorted the evidence. According to the former dean, Mr. Carson denied King's plagiarisms to Mr. Westling "unambiguously," and apparently this is where the latter got the notion that "not a single instance" of plagiarism is evident in any of the 343 pages of King's dissertation.

In fact, even after the King plagiarism story broke, even after admitting that King plagiarized far more than just his doctoral dissertation, Mr. Carson continued his campaign of deception and distortion. An article in the November/December 1990 *Stanford Observer* quotes him as saying "his [King's] professors did not expect originality in his compositions." Surely *Dr.* Carson, Ph.D., knows that the chief requirement of a doctoral dissertation is that it constitute an original contribution to scholarship.

Mr. Carson laid on another coat of whitewash in a January 16, 1991, article in the *Chronicle of Higher Education*. In a tangle of half-truths and misrepresentations, Mr. Carson comes to the nub of the matter: "[King's] legitimate utilization of political, philosophical, and literary texts — particularly those expressing the nation's democratic ideals — inspired and mobilized many Americans, thereby advancing the cause of social justice." Translation: plagiarism is excusable if done for the furtherance of "good" causes. Having settled the ethical question for us, Mr. Carson then says that we are to admire "King as the pre-eminent American orator of the 20th century," even while "recognizing that textual appropriation was one aspect of a successful composition method."

Now, it has always been realized that orators and scholars do their work in a tradition in which ideas and expressions can become common property, but what would we think of, say, Edmund Burke or Abraham Lincoln if they had systematically attempted to pass off the work of others as their own? We may still consider them great men of historical significance, even wonderful public speakers, but would not this revelation tarnish how we judge "their" rhetoric, their "composition method," and taint — ever so slightly — how we view their character? David Garrow, the Pulitzer Prize-winning author of *Bearing the Cross: Martin Luther King, Jr., and the Southern Leadership Crisis*, seems to think so. As he told the *New York Times* on November 10, 1990, the overwhelming evidence of King's plagiarisms "has altered my judgment of him as a person, though it hasn't shaken my tremendous regard for his courage and dedication to his movement." Nationally syndicated columnist William Raspberry agreed. "I have used [King's] example to impress on young people the value of scholarship," he wrote on November 17, 1990, "and to tell them (and myself) that intellectual integrity is no less valuable than physical courage. So it cannot be inconsequential that his scholarship and his intellectual integrity are now called into question. In one area . . . my hero has let me down." So can a cultural hero be worthy of respect and not reverence? Garrow and Raspberry would apparently say yes.

Also, what if, in composing the Gettysburg Address — one of the most seminal speeches in American history — Lincoln had stolen the words of a then-unknown black man, slave or free? Would we still simply conclude, as apologists have with regard to King's plagiarisms, that what is important is not where Lincoln got his words but how he "inspired and mobilized many Americans, thereby advancing the cause of social justice"? Would this, *really*, be the end of the story?

Mr. Muelder's letter also clarified something about Jon Westling of Boston University: it revealed the seriousness with which Mr. Westling viewed this matter. As the former dean explained, after John Reed's letter, Mr. Westling contacted Mr. Muelder and had the latter contact Mr. S. Paul Schilling of Maryland, the second "reader" of King's dissertation. Mr. Westling then contacted Mrs. King and the King Center in Atlanta and Clayborne Carson at Stanford, wrote John Reed in North Carolina, and even felt the need to address the "false story" of King's plagiarism, which by his own admission was spreading "like whooping cough among the unvaccinated," by writing *Chronicles* the now infamous October 5 letter that denied King's plagiary. Mr. Westling obviously ran up a lot of phone bills and used a lot of stamps.

Why, then, if Mr. Westling so clearly understood the seriousness of this matter and the serious repercussions that such a story could have for the reputation of the university he represents, did he rely exclusively on information from outside sources, some of whom might have an obvious interest in seeing such a charge denied and such a story suppressed for as long as possible? Why, in other words, did he do everything but the simplest and most logical and conclusive action of all, that of picking up the theses and examining the evidence for himself? Or why did he not have an aide, or his theology department, do it for him? After all, he and Boston University were in the best position of anyone to either deny or substantiate the validity of the charge. Boston University is the only university in the world that has both King's and Boozer's dissertations.

Mr. Westling has floated several excuses to justify his actions. His plea to the *Chicago Tribune* was that "I'm just an academic administrator trying to keep the story straight." Westling apparently is even trying to discredit *Chronicles* by telling folks that we sat on the evidence of King's plagiarisms and deliberately delayed our story all in an effort to make him look bad. First, we had never even heard of Jon Westling until he wrote us. Second, we received a copy of Boozer's dissertation a mere two weeks before Mr. Westling sent us his *unsolicited* letter, and received Boozer's actual dissertation from B.U.'s Interlibrary Loan Department only four days before; his library would be happy to substantiate these facts. A first draft of my article was completed within two weeks of receiving the evidence, which then began the three-month publishing process through which all *Chronicles* articles must pass. Mr. Westling's bizarre conspiracy theory and inflated sense of his own importance are stories in themselves.

Mr. Westling, in fact, seems congenitally incapable of staying out of hot water, as recent mishaps prove once again. As the current president of Boston University, Westling has crusaded against granting social services to "special needs" students, such as those suffering from dyslexia and attention deficit disorder. To show how absurd the demands of the learning disabled have become, he has frequently highlighted the case of "Somnolent Samantha," a student who reportedly demanded extra help from the university because she suffered an inability to stay awake in class. Well, under cross-examination in April 1997 as part of a lawsuit from students legitimately suffering from such illnesses, Westling admitted that "Somnolent Samantha" does not really exist. "What I was doing here was creating a persona," he explained, "a fictional persona who allowed me a way into the broader subject that I wanted to cover." If Westling is really just a straight-shooting bureaucrat — "just an academic administrator trying to keep the story straight" — then lying seems a dubious way of making this case.

In the end, Boston University had the opportunity to control the cards in the King plagiarism matter, but Jon Westling gave away the game. By placing his and his university's reputation in the hands of Clayborne Carson and his coterie at the King Papers Project, Mr. Westling earned the dunce cap awarded him by James Warren of the *Chicago Tribune* (November 18, 1990).

AS WE now know, thanks to Charles Babington's January 28, 1991, article in the *New Republic*, several major publications — such as the *Washington Post, the New York Times, the Atlanta Journal/Constitution*, and the *New Republic* itself (it is commendable that the *New Republic* can stand some self-criticism) — knew the facts of this story but refused to publish them. And the publications that have actually reported this story have been busy at spin control ever since.

Take the *New York Times* and the *Wall Street Journal*, for example. After the *Time*'s initial report on the King plagiarism story, it then softened the blow a few days later with a puff-ball editorial pooh-poohing the controversy. After all, it editorialized on November 13, 1990, John Kennedy had his Theodore Sorensen, George Bush his Peggy Noonan — as if taking someone's work without permission and then claiming it as your own is somehow equivalent to the work of a paid speechwriter. The *Wall Street Journal's* backpedaling was even more embarrassing. The *Journal* reported the plagiarism on November 9, ran a November 15 editorial that says King's plagiary does not so much reflect on the character of King as it "tells something about the rest of us," and then published a January 21 editorial by a Professor George McLean that praised King's plagiarized dissertation as "a contribution in scholarship for which his doctorate was richly deserved." Now, one may not want to strip King of his title of "doctor" at this late date, but to say that his doctorate was "richly deserved" on the very basis of his blatantly plagiarized dissertation is absurd and dishonest.

The *Journal's* coverage of this story did not go unnoticed by the London *Sunday Telegraph*, which reported: "Such is the cravenness of the U.S. media when it comes to race that no newspaper followed [our December 1989] story, until Friday. Then, in an article full of apologetic, mealy-mouthed phrases, the *Wall Street Journal* confirmed our findings." But perhaps the *Journal's* cravenness should not have surprised us. After all, the *Journal* tipped its hand in its November 15 editorial, when it stressed the importance of covering this story in a "carefully modulated" way.

Not surprisingly, the breaking of this story sent shock waves through the King Papers Project. Most noticeably, Ralph Luker was dropped as the associate editor of the project. Clayborne Carson's staff had reportedly been in disarray for quite some time, and sources associated with the project called Luker "expendable," the "fall guy," the "sacrificial lamb" needed to get the King Papers Project back on track. It was Luker's misfortune to be editing the project's volume dealing with King's plagiarized dissertation. Sources also cited Coretta King as being "less than helpful" throughout this episode. Her refusal to release her husband's handwritten dissertation note cards reportedly strained her relations with Carson and the project, and one source even blamed her uncooperativeness for the project's delay in coming forth with the evidence of King's plagiarism. Such excuses won't wash. Mrs. King may indeed have hindered the uncovering of the truth, and note cards may be helpful in explaining how the plagiarism was conducted, but neither Mrs. King's cooperation nor the dissertation note cards were needed to substantiate King's offense.

One source attempted to defend the project's handling of this matter by arguing, "It's not the business of scholars to report politically sensitive information, that's the business of journalists." Recent history, however, does not bear this out. Innumerable scholars were involved in compiling the Kurt Waldheim dossier, and their discoveries were published as soon as they were made. Nor did the editors at the University of Nebraska Press lie about the evidence, misrepresent the facts, or attempt a cover-up of the issue — as Clayborne Carson has admittedly done — when they came upon the pro-fascist writings of Paul de Man. De Man's overeducated apologists may have tried to obscure the issue by "deconstructing" the controversy to a jejune debate over language, but the scholarly community and the mainstream press did their job nonetheless: they pursued the truth and set forth the evidence for the world to see and examine for itself.

So what could explain the academy's and mass media's schizophrenic behavior toward these similarly sensitive and explosive stories? Could the answer be that Martin Luther King, Jr., was a man of the left, while De Man and Waldheim associated with the political right? Could race and political orientation be the reasons why Boston University took nearly one year after the breaking of this story to issue a statement about King but found plenty of time to disparage and denounce its conservative Dean of Communications, Joachim Maitre, for the same offense of plagiarism? In fact, the University of Nebraska Press started editing Paul de Man's writings about the same time Clayborne Carson claims to have uncovered solid evidence of King's plagiarism, in late 1987, and by 1991 Nebraska had published two formidable books on De Man. What had Clayborne Carson accomplished during this same time? By the time the King plagiarism story broke, he had received over a half-million dollars of the taxpayers' money and published not a single volume of King's works — and the King Papers Project had been in existence for six years. The one article he wrote on the subject was rejected by the *Journal of American History* because of his lack of forthrightness with the evidence; as one source put it, Carson was asked to rewrite the article "with more of an interpretation."

Someone who did not shy away from an "interpretation" of the evidence was John Higham, Professor of History Emeritus at John Hopkins University and editor of *Civil Rights and Social Wrongs: Black-White Relations Since World War II* (1997). Higham was for many years a member of the Council and Executive Committee of the American Historical Association. His article "Habits of the Cloth and Standards of the Academy" in the special June 1991 issue of the *Journal of American History* dealing with King's plagiary argued that literary theft is more than an academic matter: it sows confusion and weakens morale in the community at large. He said King, "the greatest modern spokesman for rights," failed a test of responsibility, and that the American historical associations — by refusing to uphold the standards of their craft — are failing as well. His article follows:

The case of Martin Luther King, Jr., challenges our understanding of plagiarism and our will to resist its multitudinous
forms, one and all, while distinguishing among them. Unfortunately, there cannot be the slightest doubt that in his student
days King became a confirmed plagiarist. The early Boston
University paper "Contemporary Continental Theology" is fes-
tooned with page references to European texts. Not only the
passages purportedly quoted from those texts but also the sur-
rounding expository phraseology derive from successive pages
in the work of a major American interpreter. As practical plagiarists do, King occasionally simplified the phraseology of the
book by Walter Marshall Horton that he was relying on. Yet
the poetry of Horton's exegesis could prove irresistible. I find
particularly disheartening King's unacknowledged appropriation of Horton's beautiful description of Platonic love: "led up
and away from the world, on wings of aspiration, beyond all
transient things and persons."

How could King's professor have failed to notice the blatantly unoriginal character of this paper? It certainly violated
the then-prevailing standards for students at every level, as I
remember from particular incidents in survey courses that I
and other young instructors were teaching at the time at the
University of California, Los Angeles (UCLA) and Rutgers
University. We were vigilant about just such papers. Our teaching assistants were asked to be equally so. On the other hand,
a few of the older faculty at UCLA were shockingly lax, particularly in dealing with a favored group such as varsity ath-
letes. Could King's teacher, presumably L. Harold DeWolf, have

been too busy or too lazy to read the paper carefully? Could he have assigned it a grade on the basis of his personal impression of an obviously ambitious, intelligent, and attractive student? Or could DeWolf, while noticing the false precocity of the paper, have held his tongue in order to gain the loyalty, or at least not impede the progress, of a black Christian rising on wings of aspiration? In either case, the professor failed in his duty to King. He owed his erring student a salutary lesson that could have added to King's ultimate stature.

By the time King wrote his doctoral dissertation, he was now in firmer possession of the texts he was construing. Doubtless he was also more confident of his own ability to organize the thoughts of difficult writers into a coherent exposition. The habit of appropriation went deep, however. It is embarrassing to discover how frequently King's doctoral dissertation adopted as his own the formulations of Paul Tillich's ideas that he found in another unpublished thesis, this one by Jack Boozer, which the estimable L. Harold DeWolf had recently supervised.

At this point one begins to wonder if King, along with fellow students and professors, was enmeshed in a subculture of tacit rhetorical license. In certain kinds of philosophy courses and especially in schools of religion, practice may have strayed farther from principle than it did elsewhere. No one can study the German philosophical tradition, for example, without discovering the extreme difficulty of rendering its metaphysical constructions faithfully into one's own language. Teachers and critics impose on all whom they grade the overriding requirement of accuracy. Getting it wrong almost certainly brings a penalty. Everyone who is cutting a path through a dense thicket of words depends therefore on precise phrasing, which often benefits from extensive quotation. Yet writers know they will appear to be not using their own conceptualizing skills if they quote "too much." The temptation can be strong to drop the quotation marks silently from time to time.

Among students of the history of philosophy, temptations of this sort could reach up to the very top of the professoriat, as the editors and staff of the Martin Luther King, Jr., Papers Project discovered in comparing John Herman Randall, Jr.'s introduction to *The Theology of Paul Tillich* with Tillich's own magnum opus, *Systematic Theology*. Training in divinity probably adds a further predisposition toward rhetorical appropriation. The emotive power of ideas must count heavily with people who embrace a clerical vocation. Although the desire to persuade infuses every kind of discourse, it is the very raison d'etre of an evangelical minister. One can well imagine a shared reluctance among teachers and students in a theological seminary to be consistently critical of their own strong urge to throw off both the hobbling of laborious paraphrase and the distancing effect of constant quotation. Still, the likely influence of a seminary subculture offers no absolution for Martin Luther King, Jr. The standards of the academy were honored at Boston University's School of Theology. Even though King's departures from those standards went almost entirely unnoticed, the second reader of the dissertation did insist that an unacknowledged quotation from Tillich be properly identified. The moral imperative for truth seeking as an open, collaborative endeavor belongs not just to its academic homeland but to every province of inquiry, and rational inquiry is what King's education at Boston University was about. Open, collaborative inquiry is the principle that defines the behavior every truth-seeking situation requires.

The chief problem in dealing with plagiarism has never been the murkiness of its parameters but rather the enforcement of its premises. The parameters *are* indistinct; they call for judgment. The premises, on the other hand, are clear. First, plagiarism obstructs the testing and validation of knowledge by hiding its true sources. Second, the plagiarist violates the code of a truth-seeking community by appropriating for himself the distinctive form in which someone else has tried to make a contribution. In both respects plagiarism sows confusion and weakens morale in the community it strikes. Yet academic institutions, publishers, and leaders have been painfully reluctant to move decisively against gross offenders.

Thomas Mallon's *Stolen Words* tells the sad story of what has become the most notorious case of academic mismanagement of plagiarism in recent years. In 1981 Jayme Sokolow was allowed to withdraw his application for tenure at Texas Tech University, without being turned down by his colleagues, after they had discovered the impressive range of his plagiarized writings. His record unblemished, Sokolow got a new job at the National Endowment for the Humanities, monitoring its grants for educational research. He proceeded, undeterred, with publication of the plagiarized book manuscript that had been his undoing in Texas. When challenged, he was then allowed to legitimize the book by sending the *American Historical Review* what seemed a handsome apology for carelessness in giving insufficient credit to another scholar. Four years later, in 1989, while the leaders of the American Historical Association (AHA) still cloaked in deepest silence the protests they were receiving concerning Sokolow's behavior, a reputable academic publisher accepted and announced for publication a second book-length manuscript by Sokolow, not knowing that it exploited another young man's research more guardedly but in similar ways.

Why do responsible scholars and administrators shrink from their clear obligation to uphold within their chosen profession the standards of the academy? The generally acknowledged cause is fear of being sued for libel. In itself a sensible concern, that has become a vastly overblown rationalization for other inhibitions that most of us are less willing to admit. There are good ways of dealing with the threat of litigation if it arises in a profession whose members know what they stand for. This fear should no longer palsy the AHA or intimidate individual complainants.

What really checks enforcement, in my view, are two wider constraints. One is a long-standing preoccupation of scholarly organizations with rights and a concomitantly casual attitude toward responsibilities. The other, interlocking with the first, is the self-interested cynicism of our age, which says in effect that we are all phonies, that ambition deserves a certain latitude, that the "rat race" forces people to cut corners, and that self-righteous whistleblowers only make trouble.

In 1985, after co-authoring an official statement on plagiarism at the request of the Council of the AHA, I wrote the following to the vice-president of the Professional Division about how that statement should be enforced:

"We all need to appreciate that the Professional Division of the AHA, like the AAUP, has seen itself as a champion of the rights of scholars against external threats and constraints. It has not concerned itself in a serious, sustained way with the responsibilities of historians although it is the obvious place for that concern to be located. I believe that we have moved into an era in which the advancement of the profession depends more on upholding our responsibilities than it does on defending rights, important and vital though the latter will always be.

"The crux of my part of the plagiarism statement was an insistence on publicity. The best thing the AHA could do to uphold ethical standards, I believe, would be to open a space in the [AHA] newsletter in which alleged violations of those standards are conscientiously reported, including the outcome."

Four years later I wrote again to the vice-president of the Professional Division: "Statements of principle merely camouflage reality unless they are applied; and the application in this area for which we, the historical profession, are responsible is publicity."

Nevertheless, the policy of silence remains in force. The AHA has become more active in investigating complaints, and in December 1989 it lifted a total prohibition on revealing the outcome of individual cases. At the present writing, however, the organization still resists disclosure of specific names or circumstances.

In this context the discovery of Martin Luther King, Jr.'s academic transgressions seems, at first glance, to present still another obstacle to moral clarity and collective resolve. The greatest modern American spokesman for rights failed a test of responsibility, from which no historian can grant exceptions without compromising the integrity of his own vocation. Yet many of us, and millions more beyond our ranks, will be tempted by the example of a hero to take more lightly the responsibility for full intellectual disclosure.

The process of converting King's blemish into a grand achievement has in fact already begun. Keith D. Miller has discovered that King misled most of his biographers and admirers when he claimed in an autobiographical essay that his civil rights leadership was inspired by his own study of great philosophers, theologians, and social thinkers. In specifying the challenge that intellectual giants such as Mahatma Gandhi, Karl Marx, and Reinhold Niebuhr offered him, King "borrowed" the words and thoughts of seven of his own teachers and friends — all of whom went entirely unmentioned. Miller uses this revelation not to raise but to *dismiss* the issue of plagiarism. The wellspring of King's thought, according to Miller, was neither the great white and Asian thinkers whom King cited nor the less prestigious associates whom he ignored but rather the oral culture of the traditional black church, in which borrowing and repetition sustain a communal merging of identities. Miller concludes that King's "remarkable ability to mine and to weld other writers' discourse" enabled him to construct a "philosophical persona" that was essential to his success in attracting white audiences. Such audiences, Miller wants us to suppose, "would not have responded favorably to a straightforward tribute to his father and his community."

Miller offers a powerful explanation of King's rhetorical prowess, but in doing so he disregards the moral obtuseness that a "philosophical persona" concealed. The oral culture of the black church certainly did not compel King to ignore the primary influence of his father or to exploit the writings of his teachers. The Miller thesis does nothing to teach our students that prophets of social justice are often insensitive to their own injustice to individuals on whom they depend.

CHAPTER FIVE

HOUDINIS OF TIME

The *Wall Street Journal* once said that it was important to cover the King plagiarism story in a "carefully modulated" way, and "carefully modulated" is the best way to describe the book industry's approach to this story. Clayborne Carson's *The Papers of Martin Luther King, Jr. Volume I: Called to Serve, January 1929 – June 1951* (University of California Press) and Keith Miller's *Voice of Deliverance: The Language of Martin Luther King, Jr. and Its Sources* (Free Press) were both published in 1992. Though invaluable for tracing the sources of King's writings and rhetoric, both books remain prime examples of academic "spin control."

It took Clayborne Carson seven years on public and private payrolls as senior editor of the King Papers Project to produce the first volume of MLK's papers. If Professor Carson had been candid with the public from the very beginning of this controversy, the long delay in publishing the first volume might be excused and justified. After all, the thousands of plagiarized passages in King's sermons, speeches, college papers, seminary essays, doctoral dissertation, and published articles could so overwhelm an editor that a plea for patience might be understandable. But Carson chose duplicity over disclosure, opting to misrepresent the facts, hide the truth as long as possible, and then whitewash the evidence after the story broke.

As the reader will see, Carson is finally earning his pay as a public servant and identifying the sources of King's writings. Carson's interpretation of the evidence, however, is disingenuous at best if not intentionally misleading, which only diminishes the quality of his exhaustively researched book. If Carson is too much the scholar not to set forth the evidence of King's plagiary — better late than never — he is too much an apologist for King not to let the evidence simply speak for itself.

Volume one documents the period from King's birth to his application to the doctoral program at Boston University and summarizes his family history in an introduction by the volume editors. King was born in Atlanta, Georgia, in 1929, the son of the revered pastor of Ebenezer Baptist Church. After attending a number of schools in Atlanta, he passed a special examination in 1944 to enter Morehouse College without having earned his high school diploma. He graduated in 1948 with a degree in sociology and entered the Crozer Theological Seminary in Chester, Pennsylvania. Obtaining his bachelor's degree in divinity in 1951, he then enrolled in the doctoral program at B.U.'s School of Theology.

King was reared, in his own words, "in a very congenial home situation," with parents who "always lived together very intimately." Closest to him was his maternal grandmother, whose death in 1941 left him emotionally unstable. Remorseful because he had learned of her fatal heart attack while attending a parade without his parents' permission, the 12-year-old Martin attempted suicide by jumping from a second-story window.

Most striking about the Kings is the affluence they enjoyed during the Depression. As King, Sr., admitted, "the deacons took great pride in knowing that [he] was the best-paid Negro minister in the city." In fact, while millions of white and black Americans were queuing in bread lines, King, Sr., was touring France, Italy, Germany, and the Holy Land. Though he refused to join the migration to the more prestigious areas of Atlanta to which middle- and upper-middle-class blacks like himself were then moving, King's father did buy a larger home in his same neighborhood, "thus fulfilling a childhood ambition of King, Sr., to own such a house. Enjoying the benefits of his family's affluence, King, Jr., became active in the social life of middle-class Atlanta."

The key phrase above reads not "middle-class black Atlanta" but simply "middle-class Atlanta," and it was the bourgeois culture of white America that shaped King's early adult years. When King entered the Crozer Theological Seminary in 1948, he was one of only 11 black students of a student body nearing a hundred. He immersed himself "in the social and intellectual life of a predominantly white, northern seminary," and "most accounts of King's experiences at Crozer suggest that he actively sought out social contacts with white students and faculty members." Known for his wonderful oratorical skills, King became one of the most popular students on campus and was even elected president of the student body, a feat that did not go unnoticed among the faculty and administration. As Crozer's Professor Morton Enslin wrote in his letter of recommendation for King to B.U.,

> The fact that with our student body largely Southern in constitution a colored man should be elected to and be popular [in] such a position is in itself no mean recommendation. The comparatively small number of forward-looking and thoroughly trained Negro leaders is, as I am sure you will agree, still so small that it is more than an even chance that one as adequately trained as King will find ample opportunity for useful service. He is entirely free from those somewhat annoying quali-

ties which some men of his race acquire when they find them-selves in the distinct higher percent of their group.

King's eagerness and ability to mix well with white students becomes significant when seen in light of his performance during Crozer's field-work program. On the basis of King's preaching to black congregations, the evaluator of the program, the Reverend William E. Gardner — who was also a friend of the King family — determined Martin's "strongest points" to be his "clarity of expression, impressive personality," his chief weakness "an attitude of aloofness, disdain and possible snobbishness which prevent his coming to close grips with the rank and file of ordinary people. Also, a smugness that refuses to adapt itself to the demands of ministering effectively to the average Negro congregation."

The editors conclude from this that King had "become somewhat es-tranged from his Ebenezer roots." Perhaps, but other evidence presented by the editors suggests that King may have inherited the class conscious-ness characteristic of his family. The editors admit in the introduction that Martin's grandfather, A.D. Williams, had made money off a contro-versial business venture that targeted poor blacks. The black-run *Atlanta Independent* in 1909 called the stock that Williams was selling in a Mexi-can silver mine a "fake, pure and simple," and encouraged him "to ex-plain . . . this fraudulent scheme" to the "many thousands of poor Ne-groes that are being defrauded throughout the state."

As Professor Enslin's letter to B.U. suggests, King was recommended for doctoral studies for reasons other than intellectual distinction and academic achievement. In fact, we know from King's scores on the Graduate Record Exam that he scored in the second lowest quartile in English and vocabulary, in the lowest ten percent in quantitative analysis, and in the lowest third on his advanced test in philosophy — a subject critical to the topic of his doctoral thesis. Instead, King was recommended for doctoral studies because he socialized well with white students, had won white support and approval, could be of "useful service" in the future, and, so far from displaying any of those "annoying qualities" that other Negroes exhibited (whatever this means), had even showed a disdain toward Negroes of a lower socioeconomic order. It was clearly on the basis of race and class, not scholarship, that Enslin recommended King for doctoral studies.

The possibility that King benefited from white paternalism or from an early form of affirmative action — from a lowering of academic standards or from preferential treatment because of his race — gains credence when his years of plagiarizing are considered. Though the editors treat this issue as gingerly as possible, their volume clearly proves that King was an inveterate plagiarist who began pilfering at an early age. The seminal speech he gave in Atlanta at the age of 15 is not only, as the editors say, "more polished than other pieces that King wrote as a teenager," it is perhaps more polished than anything King produced in either college or the seminary. The editors conclude that the "essay probably benefited from adult editing and from King's awareness of similar orations." Put less charitably, the speech was either written by an adult or copped from an unknown source.

The evidence of King's pilferage is overwhelming. The editors do not highlight the "borrowed" sections but simply reprint in footnotes the original passages King plagiarized, making the footnotes in this volume often as long and tedious as the documents themselves. From King's essay on "Ritual," written as a junior or senior at Morehouse College:

King:

All feasts are divided into
two classes, feasts of precept
and feasts of devotion.
The feasts of precept are
holydays [sic] on which the
Faithful in most Catholic
countries refrain from un-
necessary servile labor and
attend Mass. These include
all the Sundays in the year,
Christmas Day, the
circumcism [sic] . . .

Plagiarized source:

All feasts are divided into
two classes, feasts of precept
and feasts of devotion.
The former are
holy days on which the
Faithful in most Catholic
countries refrain from un-
necessary servile labour and
attend Mass. These include
all the Sundays in the year,
Christmas Day, the
Circumcision . . .

From King's essay on "The Significant Contributions of Jeremiah
to Religious Thought," written during his first term at Crozer:

King:

This Temple was the
pivot of the nation's religion. It was a national
institution, linked intimately with the fortunes of the
race. In the course of
years elaborate
ceremonies were
enacted, and the
priests prescribed sacrifices,
and the smoke of burnt-
offerings rose high from the

Plagiarized source:

[The Temple] was the . . .
pivot of the nation's religion. . . . It was a national
institution, linked intimately with the fortunes of the
race. . . . In the course of
centuries an elaborate litur-
gical ceremony came to be
enacted there, and the
priests prescribed sacrifices,
and the smoke of burnt-
offerings rose high from the

altar. The Temple was the apple of the people's eye. To criticise [sic] it was to set aflame the fires of both religion and patriotism. And this was the very thing that Jeremiah did.	altar. . . . The Temple was the apple of the people's eye. To touch it was to set aflame the fires of both religion and patriotism. And this was just the very thing that the prophet did.

King's plagiarisms are easy to detect because their style rises above the level of pedestrian student prose. In general, if the sentences are eloquent or witty or contain allusions, analogies, metaphors, or similes, it is safe to assume that the section has been purloined. "To set aflame the fires of religion and patriotism," "It was the eye of Yahweh that was forever searching the thoughts and intents of the heart," "Evil is the Satan that laughs at logic," "Religion [is] the response of the heart to the voice of God" — all are flags of King's "textual appropriations."

King's plagiarisms grow more sweeping with each year he progresses in higher education. For instance, in his essay on "A Study of Mithraism," which he "composed" during his second year at Crozer, King lifts verbatim entire paragraphs from Franz Cumont's well-known *The Mysteries of Mithra* and W.R. Halliday's *The Pagan Background of Early Christianity*. Also evident in this essay is King's fondness for plagiarizing himself, meaning his recycling verbatim into "new" essays huge sections of compositions he had written in previous years for other classes. Amazingly, there is no evidence that King's professors ever caught on to any of this.

Particularly embarrassing are the plagiarisms King committed in his last two years in the seminary, in particular in the papers that King had composed for Professor George Washington Davis. Carson and company see nothing unusual in the fact that King took *nine* courses from this professor, because "so theologically compatible were King and Davis" and because King "forged his own theological perspective" in Davis's courses, for which "King's essays . . . displayed a greater degree of intellectual engagement" than those he had written for other Crozer professors.

If what the editors say is true, King's compositions for Professor Davis should be the best argued, best written, most erudite and original of all his essays. The evidence suggests otherwise. From the introduction to King's "The Sources of Fundamentalism":

King:

In the course of its development western civilization has
shifted from a colonial naivete
of the frontier to the far-reach-
ing machination of national-
ism and from an agrarian
pattern of occupation to the
industrial one. . . .

Plagiarized source:

In the course of its development western civilization has
shifted from a colonial naivete
of the frontier to the far-reach-
ing machinations of national-
ism and from an agrarian
pattern of occupation to the
industrial one. . . .

Plagiarism continues throughout eight of the remaining 13 paragraphs of the essay.

From the introduction to King's "The Origin of Religion in the Race":

King:

Before we come to consider
some modern theories it
may be well to refer briefly to
two views which were once
widely prevalent, but which
are now obsolete or
at least absolescent [sic].

Plagiarized source:

Before we come to consider
some modern theories it
may be well to refer briefly to
two views which were once
widely prevalent, but which
are now obsolete or
obsolescent.

Only three of the remaining 22 paragraphs in the essay are not replete with verbatim plagiarisms, often of entire paragraphs.

From King's essay on "The Humanity and Divinity of Jesus":

King:	*Plagiarized sources:*
If there is any one thing of which modern Christians have been certain it is that Jesus was a true man, bone of our bone, flesh of our flesh, in all points tempted as we are. . . . Like the rest of us, he got hungry. When at the well of Sameria [sic] he asked the woman who was drawing water for a drink. When he grew tired, he needed rest and sleep. . . . On the Cross, he added to all physical tortures the final agony of feeling God-forsaken.	If there is any one thing of which Christians have been certain it is that Jesus is true man, bone of our bone, flesh of our flesh, in all points tempted as we are. . . . Like the rest of us, he was hungry. At the well at Samaria he asked the woman who was drawing water for a drink. When he grew tired, he needed rest and sleep. . . . On the Cross, he added to all physical tortures the final agony of feeling God-forsaken.

Regarding some of the other essays King wrote for Professor Davis, of the 37 paragraphs in his essay on "The Influence of the Mystery Religions on Christianity," 11 are recycled from two essays written in previous years and 24 of the remaining 26 paragraphs are replete with verbatim plagiarisms. In "The Origin of Religion in the Race," only four of the 24 paragraphs are free of verbatim theft. In "Religion's Answer to the Problem of Evil," only 14 of the 38 paragraphs are free of verbatim plagiarisms.

Again, Carson concludes from these "engaged" essays, which Davis routinely gave A's, and from the *nine* courses King took from Davis, that the student and the professor were merely "compatible." One could just as likely conclude that the professor had been snowed. We know from comments written on King's essays that some professors reprimanded him for incomplete footnotes, but there is no evidence to indicate that they ever realized the extent of his pilfering. Whether King's cheating slipped by intentionally or unintentionally, we will probably never know. In either case, King's teachers did him a great disservice.

The editors admit in their introduction, in classic Carsonese, that King's essays possess "unacknowledged textual appropriations," once again eschewing use of the "p-word." In fact, they say that King's "borrowings" only constitute literary theft if we use "a strict definition of plagiarism." Even then, they assure us, there is still no "definite answer to the question whether King deliberately violated the standards that applied to him as a student"! The editors of the King Papers may feign an ignorance of academic praxis and pretend not to know what a gross violation of scholarly standards would look like, but at least King himself knew. He plainly states on page seven of his dissertation, "The present inquiry will utilize from these valuable secondary sources any results which bear directly on the problem, and will indicate such use by appropriate footnotes," and then proceeds to plagiarize 33 percent of his doctoral thesis.

WHILE CARSON and his fellow apologists are making a heroic effort to palliate King's larceny, Keith Miller boldly takes the bull by the horns. Far from wanting to whitewash or trivialize the facts, Miller argues that King's pilferage was intentional, and even an integral and laudatory part of the civil rights movement. For by "voice merging" stolen texts into his speeches and essays, and by taking in particular the words of liberal white ministers, King "foolproofed his discourse" and was able to "change the minds of moderate and uncommitted whites" toward solving "the nation's most horrific problem — racial injustice."

The most useful portions of this book are those in which Miller sets forth the sources of King's nonacademic works. He occasionally mentions King's famous antiwar speeches that were ghostwritten by Andrew Young, Stanley Levison, and other supporters and aides, but he highlights the pilfered sources behind King's landmark orations on civil rights. For example, King's Nobel Prize Lecture was plagiarized extensively from works by Florida minister J. Wallace Hamilton; the sections on Gandhi and nonviolence in his "Pilgrimage" speech were taken virtually verbatim from Harris Wofford's speech on the same topic; the frequently replayed climax to the "I Have a Dream" speech — the "from every mountainside, let freedom ring" portion — came from a 1952 address to the Republican National Convention by a black preacher named Archibald Carey; and the 1968 sermon in which King prophesied his martyrdom was based on works by J. Wallace Hamilton and Methodist minister Harold Bosley.

Miller's research is indispensable for understanding King's works, but his intoxicating thesis proves fatal to his judgment:

> King's achievements are awesome. Borrowed sermons gave white Americans their best — and probably last — chance to solve what had always been the nation's worst problem. Not only did voice merging keep Jefferson's dream alive, it also helped compel the White House to withdraw from the nightmare of Vietnam. Then in the wake of his movement came the second wave of American feminism, the campaign for gay rights, and the crusade to save the environment.

All this because of plagiarism! Miller apparently believes that every social and protest movement of our time is rooted in dishonesty.

A more fundamental problem with Miller's thesis is lack of proof. He offers no documentation, confession, or interview of any sort — nothing to prove that King deliberately plagiarized white sources to garner white support for the civil rights movement. Miller explains away the plagiarism King committed throughout college, seminary, and his doctoral studies — all of which occurred, in Miller's words, before King became "the unofficial president of an oppressed people" — with his notorious "voice merging" theory, and a more condescending theory could hardly be found. For on one level Miller argues, "King's plagiarism is a black thing. You whites with your standards wouldn't understand." But the deeper implications of the theory are more sinister than this. In fact, the implications are similar to the racist and sexist assumptions underlying the left's attack on the Western canon of great literature. As Roger Kimball has pointed out, if one believes that the writings of dead white Western males are inaccessible to blacks, Hispanics, and women, then one shows little faith in these groups' intellectual abilities and "implies that the highest achievements of civilization are somehow off-limits or inaccessible to certain groups." So too with the "voice merging" theory of Keith Miller, who argues, in effect, that originality and true scholarship cannot be expected of blacks, that because of their oral traditions they cannot differentiate between the pulpit and the classroom, between Sunday sermons and professional standards, between the mores of folk art and the demands of high culture. How flattering this is to all the black doctors, black lawyers, black theologians, and black scholars who have made and continue to make their way honestly in the world.

"Sir, Hell is paved with good intentions." Samuel Johnson's admonition is an instructive rejoinder to the seemingly benevolent theories of the bumpersticker crowd on the political left. Sensitivity to cultural differences and needs — what once would have been called common decency, good manners, or Christian charity — is all fine and good, and certainly the faithful among us are called on to walk humbly with God, to deal justly and mercifully with one another, and to respect our neighbor, regardless of his race. But as Christopher Lasch has pointed out, a cultural *obsession* with sensitivity, pluralism, diversity, and minority rights

> provides no comfort when young people can't seem to learn how to read or write, when they graduate with no more than a smattering of culture, when their stock of general knowledge grows more meager every day, when they can't recognize allusions to Shakespeare or the classics or the Bible or their own country's history, when SAT scores keep falling, when American workmanship and productivity are no longer the envy of the world, and when superior education is widely cited as the reason for the economic success of countries like Japan and the former West Germany.

Miller concludes by suggesting that the country should be grateful for King's commitment to plagiarism. For stealing the works of others "let King escape the restrictions of the clock and therein become a Houdini of time. . . . This ubiquitous leader could magically advise senators, write a column, publish an essay, rally voters, placate unruly staffers, preach a sermon, and comfort a church janitor — all in a single day. . . . Barnstorming the nation as a Houdini of time became possible only because King consulted sources and thereby foolproofed his discourse." King was many things to many people, and he may well have been a master of illusion and deception, but his discourse — and Miller's — is hardly foolproof.

CHAPTER SIX

TRUTH OR CONSEQUENCES

Nietzsche believed "one may sometimes tell a lie, but the grimace that accompanies it tells the truth." If America's infatuation with lies is any indication, Nietzsche clearly underestimated the modern mastery of the straight face.

Take Boston University, for instance. Like an addicted gambler unable to cut his losses and give up the game, B.U. has kept the King plagiarism story alive with frequent attacks on its critics. Assistant Provost Peter Wood, for example, has called me in print "intellectually dishonest" for having criticized his university's handling of the King plagiarism story. He says I misrepresent the actions of then-Acting B.U. President Jon Westling, who took Clayborne Carson "at his word when he said he and his colleagues had found no evidence of plagiarism in [King's] dissertation." Westling, says Wood, even undertook "a laborious process of reviewing the dissertation to search for instances of plagiarism from an unknown source" and "found nothing to contradict Dr. Carson."

Mary McCarthy famously said of Lillian Hellman that "every word she writes is a lie, including 'and' and 'the,'" and one wonders whether the same charge holds true regarding Boston University's ever-changing explanation of how it handled the King plagiarism story. First, B.U.'s story has always been that it never tried to examine King's writings but instead relied solely on the statements of Clayborne Carson and others who flatly denied that King was a plagiarist. Now, according to Provost Wood, B.U. *did* look at the evidence and *did* try to find the plagiarisms, but failed. Mr. Wood apparently believes that he does his university credit by highlighting the ineptitude of its administration. Second, Mr. Wood calls the job of detecting the plagiarisms "laborious." To set the record straight, the task is nothing of the sort, because as Falstaff said, "His thefts were too open." And third, Mr. Wood denies that B.U. attempted to stonewall or whitewash this issue. The committee that B.U. President John Silber convened to analyze King's and Boozer's theses took until October 1991 to report its findings to the public, meaning it took Boston University nearly one year to admit what the public already knew. Moreover, in reporting the university's findings to the public, committee member John Cartwright, B.U.'s "Martin Luther King, Jr., Professor of Social Ethics," told the Associated Press — in a statement carried in the *New York Times*, our nation's paper of record, and in thousands of newspapers nationwide — that there is no "blatancy" in King's plagiary and that "there is no obvious indication in [King's] dissertation that he inappropriately utilized material"! A better example of whitewashing — some would call it something else — could hardly be found.

It was B.U.'s reputation, not Mr. King's, that was riding on the committee's handling of this controversy. We all know what King did, both good and bad; the only question was whether B.U. as an institution devoted to the pursuit of truth would have the honesty and integrity to admit its mistakes and acknowledge King's wrongdoings. Mr. Wood and Mr. Cartwright tell us the answer is no.

Meanwhile, that Sinon of the professoriat, Keith Miller of Arizona State University, continues to push his Trojan hobbyhorse through the gates of academe with subversive drivel about "voice merging" in the *Chronicle of Higher Education* and elsewhere. Considering the disingenuousness with which the scholarly community has greeted the news of King's brigandry, Miller's continued push for a kinder and gentler definition of plagiarism in light of King's actions is not surprising. In fact, Miller's defense of King and his novel approach to plagiarism are both predictable. As we have learned from the frontlines of the Culture War, polygamy, female circumcision, animal sacrifices, and witchcraft are all acceptable so long as they are practices of preferred minorities, and if King committed what Samuel Johnson called "one of the most reproachful" literary crimes, then there must be something wrong with our culture's conception of theft. This bizarre logic and moral torpitude are today par for the course. Nationally syndicated columnist John Leo, in the *Washington Times* of July 27, 1997, highlighted the case of an outraged teacher whose students at Pasadena City College could write "passionately of saving the whales, of concern for the rain forest, of the rescue and tender care of a stray dog" but could not find the moral courage to condemn human sacrifices. After all, one student argued, such sacrifices might be part of a religion of "long standing."

But to Miller's chagrin, what's good for the goose is apparently not also good for the gander. The case of Bertolt Brecht is instructive here. Though he liberally stole the work of others (especially the work of his girlfriends) and, according to Kenneth Tynan, "positively welcomed the charge of plagiarism, retorting that in literature, as in life, he rejected the idea of private property," Brecht ironically fought tooth and nail to prevent communist publishing houses from securing the copyrights to his work. As R.J. Stove explained in "Mack the Thief" in Australia's *News Weekly*, "Brecht demanded — and obtained — the lavish remuneration for 'his' published utterances which only capitalist firms in the West could guarantee him." King acted similarly, as copyright expert Robert Cassler points out in the February 24, 1993, issue of the *Chronicle of Higher Education*: "Dr. King vigorously defended his copyright in 'I Have a Dream' when others wanted to use it. (See *King v. Mister Maestro, Inc.* . . . 1963)." Just as Brecht copyrighted material he took and published as his own, so King, in this case, copyrighted material he took from a black preacher named Archibald Carey. The point is this: Keith Miller and his epigones might not be interested in intellectual property rights, but King surely was.

In better days, the follies of our heroes did not move us to subvert the moral underpinnings of our culture. Great falls were lamented but expected of Fallen Man; they were the unavoidable acts in the tragedy of life, and the lessons they taught formed the grist of our greatest literature. But a rhetoric of accountability has little appeal today and pales before the lure of "diseases," "addictions," and novel theories of human behavior that conveniently exonerate us from responsibility for our actions and from the responsibility of facing our problems head-on. Just take another pill, pass another law, build another prison, or plead helpless before the evils of the affliction of the month — all are part of our obsession with quick-fix solutions and explanations of human vice.

To a certain extent, this is not surprising. America has always had trouble facing the brute facts of life. We like to abstract our past and sentimentalize our present because it allows us to linger in escapist reverie, avoiding tough questions, tough problems, and any glimpse of the horrors and heartache that make up human existence. But as St. Paul predicted, whenever the search for diversion grows too strident, "when people will not endure sound teaching, they will accumulate for themselves teachers to suit their own liking, and will turn away from listening to the truth and wander into myths." And those wandering into myths are legion today.

Marion Barry, for example, when caught cavorting with drug dealers and smoking crack cocaine while mayor of D.C., did not let down his constituency, make a mockery of political office, shirk his responsibilities, break laws, to say nothing of trivializing the real problems plaguing the black community. No, he simply had an addiction and needed a few months of counseling to build his self-esteem. Baseball star Wade Boggs, who blubbered on national television that he was "addicted to sex," did not lie to his wife, neglect his children, and cheat his teammates and his fans by playing ball only halfheartedly when his wife rather than his mistress was watching from the stands; his "disease" did. And similarly with King. He did not take the words of others and claim them as his own; no, he simply acted within a rich but little appreciated tradition to which society must learn to be sensitive.

Keith Miller; Boston University's Jon Westling, John Silber, and Peter Wood; and all but one member of the committee that B.U. convened to examine King's doctoral dissertation — all are white, which is not an inconsequential fact. For it is not blacks who have led the fight to palliate King's plagiarisms but whites, and whites of all political stripes. It is King's white apologists on both the political left and neoconservative right who have given new meaning to the term "whitewash," and their embarrassing exoneration of King and rationalization of his plagiarisms are more damaging to blacks than if B.U. had revoked King's doctorate. For by excusing King's pilferings — and in Miller's case, by excusing them as "a black thing" — King's apologists are telling black scholars everywhere that they should not bother doing their own work, or worse, that no black can really pull his own weight, write his own papers, or actually become a professional like white people can. When Miller argues that the accomplishments of blacks should be held to different and clearly less-demanding standards, that they should be discounted in light of the "black oral tradition," he takes a backhand to every black scholar honestly pursuing his craft.

In fact, these specious attempts to exonerate King have a familiar ring. They appear strikingly similar to the many other acts of penitence — such as affirmative action, reverse discrimination, the "race-norming" of everything from government exams to wartime medals, the public apologies for slavery, the gerrymandering of congressional districts to create "minority majorities," the teaching of Ebonics/Black English and Afrocentric lies in our public schools, the heavy-handed revisionism of historical events in our textbooks and movies, and the legitimization of the critical race theory of jurisprudence (by which black jurors are allowed to nullify laws and exonerate black criminals — who principally prey on other African-Americans — because increasing the number of black men in prison would be harmful to the black community's self-esteem) — that a guilt-ridden white community has felt duty-bound to perform in expiation of racial sins, both real and imagined. Reporters were shocked to learn that a teacher had asked Chelsea Clinton, then an eighth-grader at a private school, to write a term paper on the subject, "Why I Feel Guilty Being White," but considering the climate of the times and the politicized state of public education, a more appropriate assignment could hardly be found. These acts of penitence may waft of something new, of something characteristic of our more "sensitive" and enlightened present, but they just as surely smack of something very old, something redolent of the very age we have tried to exorcise and discredit: that pernicious form of paternalism called the "white man's burden" that breeds lies and deceptions and that oppresses the very people intended to be uplifted.

This "whitewash" of King's actions has many antecedents. It was the white media that appointed Jesse Jackson over Ralph Abernathy to succeed King at the head of the civil rights movement. They were the ones who publicized Jackson's lies about cradling the dying King, who published the photographs of the bogus bloody shirt, and who since then have buried all mention of this crass opportunism for which King's closest followers never forgave Jackson. Philip Nobile, whose exposé in the *Village Voice* (February 23, 1993) revealed the extent to which Alex Haley plagiarized and fabricated his "autobiography" *Roots*, reminds us that it was an all-white, 17-man jury that awarded Haley the Pulitzer Prize for his stolen work of fiction. (Haley paid a $650,000 settlement in an unpublicized plagiarism suit shortly before he died.) "If we blew the Haley prize, as we apparently did, I feel bad," William McGill — former president of Columbia University and an ex officio presence on the 1977 Pulitzer Prize board — told Nobile. "The answer to that question [whether race affected the board's decision] is yes. . . . We all labored under the delusion that sudden expressions of love could make up for historical mistakes. . . . Of course, that's inverse racism."

In fact, Nobile told *Publishers Weekly* (October 6, 1997) that Haley plagiarized "most" of *Roots*, that "virtually everything was taken from somewhere else," that the "epilogue contains lies about [the book's] preparation," and that most of Haley's writings, including his *Playboy* interviews and *The Autobiography of Malcolm X*, had been "written or mostly rewritten by others." "If [the editors at Doubleday, the publisher of *Roots*] didn't know [about the plagiarism] before," said Nobile, "they knew after publication, and the book has never been withdrawn. Its resonance in the culture is an artifact of hype." Nobile's assertions were dismissed by Doubleday as "a literary lynching" but supported by a BBC documentary called *The Roots of Alex Haley*, which aired in Great Britain in the fall of 1997. As Judge Robert Ward, who presided over Haley's plagiarism trial, concluded in the film, "Haley perpetrated a hoax on the public." Not surprisingly, there was no announcement of plans to air this documentary in America.

Race-baiting hustlers like Malcolm X — "hustler" being Malcolm's description of himself in his "autobiography," "written" by Alex Haley (if Malcolm didn't write it, Haley didn't write it, who, pray tell, finally wrote this screed?!); puffed-up poseurs like the Reverend Al Sharpton, who still claims Tawana Brawley was molested by white racists; and murdering thugs like boxing promoter Don King, who reportedly ingratiates himself with the poor inner-city youth whom he intends to exploit by distributing copies of a book called *Countering the Conspiracy to Destroy Black Boys* — all are largely the creation of white hype. As is the infamous film on World War II by Nina Rosenblum and William Miles called *The Liberators*, which purports that the "true" liberator of Hitler's most notorious concentration camps was an all-black unit of the U.S. Army. PBS televised the film nationally and hailed it as an invaluable look at a shamefully neglected aspect of world history; Hollywood plugged it as the "best documentary of the year" and quickly nominated it for an Academy Award; and yet the film has been quietly pulled from circulation, as even black veterans from the very unit supposedly responsible for the liberations have denounced it as balderdash and blatant propaganda.

Clearly such balderdash stems from whites wanting to prove their worth before the gods of sensitivity and egalitarianism. But what is lost in their effort is truth, and more often than not, the lies and myths substituted for truth only harm the very people intended to be helped by these lies and myths. "White college presidents routinely lie about the racial double standards that exist from coast to coast," wrote Thomas Sowell in *Human Events* (July 4, 1997). But by doing so, they set "up high rates of failure among black college students who could be successful if they entered colleges where they meet the normal requirements. People loudly claim that test scores and academic records are not accurate predictors for minority students — even though study after study shows the opposite."

The myths and lies passing for history and fact in the Afrocentric Baseline Essays — which purport, among other things, that Cleopatra was a "sister" and that Pythagoras and Aristotle stole their mathematics and philosophy from black scholars in Egypt — are also prime examples of lies that only fuel blacks' anxiety, feed their hatred of the majority culture, and exacerbate their despair and delusions of helplessness. Look at the Baseline Essay on science and technology which Arthur Schlesinger, Jr., highlighted in *The Disuniting of American* (1991). According to Afrocentric mythology, when black American scientist Charles Drew, who developed the first successful process for preserving blood plasma, was seriously injured in a 1950 automobile accident in North Carolina, and was losing great quantities of blood, "*Not one* of several nearby white hospitals would provide the blood transfusions he so desparately [sic] needed, and on the way to a hospital that treated Black people, he died." As Schlesinger notes, this is "a hell of a story — the inventor of blood-plasma storage dead because racist whites denied him his own invention. Only it is not true." According to the biographical essay on Drew written by black scholar Rayford Logan for the *Dictionary of American Negro Biography*, "Conflicting versions to the contrary, Drew received prompt medical attention."

These lies often make "a hell of a story," as the church burning hoax has demonstrated in recent years. Though even the Clinton administration's National Church Arson Task Force had to admit last year that more white than black churches suffered arson in 1996 — that only *two or three* out of 199 suspected arsons had links to white supremacist groups — the facts of this case did not prevent the Center for Democratic Renewal, the National Council of Churches, the Christian Coalition, Promise Keepers, and the National Association of Evangelicals from playing the race card and raising millions of dollars to fight this bogus rash of racially-motivated torchings. Leona Helmsley herself, the "Queen of Mean" who is searching for redemption, donated $1 million to the NCC's Burned Churches Fund. As Mark Tooley of the Institute on Religion and Democracy reported in November 1997, "Having raised over $11 million in total, the NCC and the CDR have little reason to admit that their claims about church arson as an emblem of surging American racism have not withstood close scrutiny."

Unfortunately, few news stories today or claims from the academy can withstand close scrutiny.

CHAPTER SEVEN

SCHOLARSHIP AND THE KING LEGACY

The following sections from Eugene Genovese's *Southern Front: History and Politics in the Culture War* (University of Missouri Press, 1995) constitute the best analysis to date of the significance of King's scholarship to his theology and political philosophy. They discuss King's many weaknesses as a scholar and place his plagiary in the context of his legacy.

King's stature as an American and world-historical, as well as a discretely black, political leader remains secure. No amount of idol-smashing is likely to dim his luster. Our immense debt to the man and our respect for his memory do not, however, provide the slightest excuse for a political agenda that credits him with virtues he did not have and successes he did not achieve. Historians, at least those not mesmerized by postmodernist claptrap, ought to know that sooner or later the truth will out.

In the long run, King's personal and professional lapses are not likely to diminish his stature any more than assorted revelations are likely to diminish significantly the stature of others who deserve to be revered as constructive historical figures. Great men, more often than not, commit great sins and must be prepared, even more readily than others, to go to their death as Pushkin's Boris Goudonov went to his, crying out, "Forgive a poor sinner." The unfolding tragedy lies elsewhere. Those who foolishly think they protect his memory by denying or explaining away his lapses from his own highest moral standards render difficult a sober assessment of his legacy.

The scandal of King's well-documented plagiarism reveals only part of the even greater scandal of an academic career that will not bear scrutiny. Theodore Pappas has chronicled that scandal and the even worse scandal of the reaction of the media and academia in *The Martin Luther King, Jr., Plagiarism Story* (1994), which deserves much more attention than it has been getting. There is a curious feature to King's plagiarism — and other cheating — for he constantly wrestled with difficult subject matter. The laziness and indifference that usually mark plagiarists do not seem to have been at issue here. From his undergraduate days he displayed a deep thirst for a knowledge of God, making a constant effort to understand God's nature and his will. Plagiarized or no, his papers, from Morehouse to Crozer to Boston University, provide ample evidence that he was thinking hard and trying to find Christian ground on which to stand. The plagiarism, that is, consisted of his collecting other people's words and thoughts to buttress a viewpoint that he was formulating through a good deal of work and reflection. It is noteworthy that King passed over the chance to take courses on social Christianity, Gandhi, race relations, and other trendy subjects, preferring courses on Plato, Hegel, formal logic, and modern philosophy. It is also noteworthy that he was active in the black students' Dialectical Society at Boston, which met regularly for what appears to have been intellectually demanding work.

In any case, King's student papers and doctoral dissertation remain required reading for those who would understand his life's work. For the moment, forget the plagiarism and the many jejune formulations of his student papers. After all, how many among us would want our graduate school papers read today? I doubt that I am alone in having burned mine. What remains striking is the extent to which the essentials of his early theological and philosophical ideas survived to influence his religio-political course to the very end. Those ideas, honed by experience and maturity, proved a tower of strength, as well as a source of some dangerous weaknesses.

In struggling to understand God, King focused on the work of those liberal theologians who bent theology to the exigencies of philosophy. Too bad. For a religion based on the relation of each individual to a God who has promised to render judgment cannot readily surrender its theology (its basic concepts of God, nature, man, sin, and salvation) to a discipline based solely on human reason. I do not mean to suggest that theologians may proceed in a manner indifferent to philosophy and human reason. The best and most "orthodox" of theologians do not make that mistake. Karl Barth, among the neo-orthodox theologians of King's day, was suspicious of the claims of philosophy, but, when push came to shove, even he had to make an attempt at constructive engagement. In any case, Christians may argue endlessly over the specific meaning of the Word, but when, as is now the fashion, they are brought to question whether the Word, as manifested in the Bible, constitutes revealed Truth, they run the grave risk of restricting themselves to arbitrary ethical pronouncements that atheists could readily share. At that point they no longer have much if anything to contribute specifically as Christians. For King, as for others, political consequences follow.

On the plagiarism: no explanations, qualifications, or fancy interpretations can excuse or mitigate it. King wrote the dissertation while he was meeting heavy responsibilities as the full-time pastor of Montgomery's prestigious Dexter Avenue Baptist Church and he encountered the temptation to cut every corner. But nothing required him to do so, and he was at his most eloquent when preaching the example of Jesus' resistance to temptation and excoriating those who lived by what he sardonically referred to as the Eleventh Commandment, "Don't get caught."

Nor will the plea that the "black sermonic tradition" permits extensive borrowing without attribution serve, for it comes a cropper of the obvious objection that the same plea might be made for the "white sermonic tradition." Since a preacher of "Christ and Him crucified" is trying to convey the Word of God, not his own words or those of another interpreter, he need cite only the Bible, which until a century or so ago American Protestant preachers could assume their parishioners knew reasonably well. At that, King sometimes stepped over the bounds of the permissible by lifting sermons virtually wholesale from others.

Whatever excuses might be made for the many liberties King took, none could possibly serve for the doctoral dissertation. By then he had been well instructed in the requisites of scholarship, including the professional norms appropriate to the critical and historical study of the interpretations of others. King clearly understood and accepted the distinction between preaching and scholarly criticism.

Although it has gone unnoticed even by King's most hostile critics, his academic career was also rife with cheating of other kinds. He pretended to have done work he clearly had not done. That, too, he got away with. Boston University has indignantly denied that its professors relaxed their standards for black students in the spirit of the racist paternalism that is now running wild on our campuses. They seem unaware that, in mounting this denial, they convict themselves of something perhaps worse — of cheating *all* students, white and black.

King barely read German, a language regarded as indispensable for serious students of theology and the language in which Tillich's early theology had been written — and not translated into English. He failed his German examination during the year in which he was taking Edgar Sheffield Brightman's seminar on Hegel. It is not even clear that King carefully studied the English translation of the crucial *Phenomenology of Mind*, for he relied heavily on W. T. Stace's *Philosophy of Hegel*, a useful book on which many of us cut our teeth as undergraduates but which can hardly substitute for a reading of Hegel. No matter. King's papers on Hegel, which his professors praised, were heavily plagiarized anyway. The dissertation cites the

German texts of Tillich's first book and other early writings, but the editors' notes show that in each case King is quoting translated passages he lifted from secondary sources.

An understanding of King's intellectual development requires a glance at the professional standards at Boston University and the temper of the leading theological seminaries of his day. L. Harold DeWolf, who took a particular interest in black students, became King's dissertation adviser when Brightman died. The editors of the King Papers remark that DeWolf and other professors had little reason to suspect plagiarism in King's papers since King did well in examinations written in class. Fair enough — so far as it goes. But we may question how responsible King's professors were in reading those papers, which were full of theological blunders. Alternatively, we may question how well grounded they themselves were in the subjects in which they purported to be specialists.

As the result of poor training, King's serious weaknesses as a student of theology become more readily explicable, although hardly excusable. King's pretense to a knowledge of German led to serious problems and claimed an especially high price in his work on the theology of Karl Barth. To make matters worse, his reading of the English translations of Barth's books was hasty and wooden. His discussion of the concept of "God as wholly other," for example, raises doubts about how well he grasped Barth's central concepts. In "Karl Barth's Conception of God," another largely plagiarized paper that won DeWolf's praise, King interpreted Barth's notion of God as "unknowable and indescribable" in a manner that reduces it to an irrationality with which Barth cannot fairly be charged. And in a thinly veiled swipe at trinitarianism, King disapprovingly quoted Barth on the personality of God without noticing Barth's implicit attack on man's egotistical attempt to make his own personality the center of all things — an attack that, in accordance with King's own views, offered a potentially solid theological basis for a radical politics.

These errors may be dismissed, if lamely, as of a kind to be expected from graduate students or as matters about which interpreters may disagree. The more serious problems concern King's and his professors' scholarly competence. In praising Barth for providing a useful counterpoint to liberal theology, King cited the English-language versions of Barth's books: *The Word of God and the Word of Man; The Knowledge of God and the Service of God; Dogmatics in Outline;* and *The Epistle to the Romans,* the second and drastically revised edition of which came as a theological thunderclap in Protestant and even Roman Catholic circles. In seminary papers and the dissertation, King attacked Barth for rejecting natural theology, and he focused on Barth's reliance on dialectical method. But by the time King was writing, Hans Urs von Balthasar's *The Theology of Karl Barth* had become available in German, as King's professors should have known, and it contained an impressive critique of Barth's rejection of natural theology that compelled a reassessment of the problem.

King's professors failed to recognize a much worse embarrassment: Barth's retreat from the dialectical method he had espoused in his *Epistle to the Romans.* They did know that Barth

had long before embarked upon what would become his magnum opus, the multivolume *Church Dogmatics* (1936-1968),
which appeared as 14 separate books, the first of which was
available in German at the time of King's work in seminary.
(Only a part of volume one had been translated.) In the 1950's,
Barth's theology was still at the center of spirited controversy
in American church circles that were reeling from, among other
crises, the departure of the orthodox Calvinists from their long-
standing stronghold at Princeton Theological Seminary.

King's professors, notably DeWolf, were keeping up with
Barth's work, but, apparently, they did not alert their students
to the problems. Calamity ensued, for Barth had radically
changed course, supplanting the dialectical method upon which
he had previously relied and on which King focused his critique. At that, King should not be criticized too severely, for
virtually every erroneous reading he made of Barth's work followed no less erroneous readings in DeWolf's own work.

Had King been subjected to the firm discipline we should
expect from theological seminaries, he might well have developed differently. But might-have-beens do not count, and King
floundered. His study of Hegel, however superficial, influenced
or reinforced his lifelong adherence to the project of subsum-
ing theology under philosophy — a project outlined in Hegel's
Early Theological Writings. King's careless treatment of Barth,
although given an A and praised as "excellent" by DeWolf,
had especially regrettable consequences, political as well as
theological and philosophical. For King ignored Barth's critique of the Hegelian project and thus bypassed the radical

left's most powerful Protestant theologian. In the event, he lost the chance to ground his politics in a more coherent and promising alternate theology.

King's discussions of Calvin contain worse embarrassments. In a paper that compared the theology of Luther and Calvin, he read Luther as stressing God's love and read Calvin as stressing His justice and power. He thereupon challenged their common emphasis on His sovereignty, insisting that "God is first and foremost an all loving Father." His professors apparently saw no need to demand that he reply to Calvinist arguments against such a dichotomy. Robert Dabney and John Girardeau, among other American Calvinists, had long before offered critiques of the dichotomy worthy of consideration, and, for whatever my opinion may be worth, they shredded it.

In seminar papers, graded high by his professors, King discusses sin and especially original sin and grossly caricatured Calvin's views: "Calvin has very little use for reason in theology formulation. He is forever speaking out against idle speculation." Calvin, the father of a school of theology that has prided itself on its appeal to reason, science, and Baconian induction, certainly did condemn "idle speculation." What estimable theologian has not? King's reading of Calvin will not inspire confidence in those who read the *Institutes of the Christian Religion* for themselves. Among other problems, he dubiously attributes supralapsarianism to Calvin and interprets it as making God responsible for the Fall and for the presence of evil in the world. Most Calvinist theologians have denied that Calvin was a supralapsarian, and all have denied that he made

God responsible for sin and evil, a charge Arminians and others have hurled not only at Calvin but at Turretin and every other Calvinist, including such Americans as Edwards, Hodge, Thornwell, Dabney, and Girardeau. At the least, students, even at an Arminian divinity school, should be required to know and evaluate the Calvinist replies.

KING NEVER did reconcile his demand for an absolute sense of right and wrong, which implied an absolute truth, with his philosophical pragmatism and his insistence that scientific thought is the measure of truth-telling in theology. Rather, he superimposed orthodox pronouncements on a liberal theology that he continued to espouse. Thus in private notes he stressed God's love as all-inclusive: "This is what distinguishes the New Testament from the Old. The God of the Old Testament was only a tribal God."

King might have pleaded that he was following in the footsteps of distinguished liberal theologians. The 19th-century New England Theology had, in effect, shunted God's justice and wrath back on the God of the Old Testament, nicely discarding the "consuming fire" and "jealous God" of Deuteronomy 4:23-24 while celebrating the love and benevolence of the God of the New Testament. And Adolph von Harnack, the renowned historian of church dogma, drove liberal theology to its logical conclusion by calling on the Christian churches to scuttle the Old Testament once and for all.

King reflected, "I have been strongly influenced by liberal theology, maintaining a healthy respect for reason and a strong belief in the immanence as well as the transcendence of God." But by 1952 he concluded that liberal theology was collapsing and that neo-orthodoxy was on the ascendant. And indeed, the assorted challenges to liberalism that were being mounted by Barth, Niebuhr, and others, whether fairly called neo-orthodoxy or no, were reemphasizing original sin and human depravity with considerable effect. King, in his notes, invoked Jeremiah and commented, "One of the great services of neo-orthodoxy, notwithstanding its extremes, is its revolt against all forms of humanistic perfectionism. They call us back to a deeper faith in God." The dissertation, then, was a culmination of King's effort, begun at Morehouse, to develop a synthesis of the best in liberal and neo-orthodox theology. Trying to find a third way, he acknowledged that he rejected neo-orthodoxy as a body of doctrine but appreciated it as a corrective for some errors in liberalism. As the editors of the King Papers acutely remark, "The significance of King's academic papers lies not in their cogency or originality, therefore, but in their reliability as expressions of his theological preferences."

King nonetheless had a hard time in living up to his own well taken strictures on the excesses of liberalism. Difficulties plagued his embrace of liberal theology, including some that had immediate political implications. King understood as much, and he struggled manfully to meet his responsibilities. Throughout his life he scoffed at the concept of a triune God, following Schleiermacher and Ritschl in viewing Jesus as a human being with "a unique and potent God consciousness." King justly considered Tillich's formal acceptance of the Trinity and a personal God as little more than the projection of a necessary fiction that could only "point to an impersonal God" and to pantheism. And he criticized Wieman for reducing God's characteristics to a minimum so low as to be beside the point. King's obsession with scientific method led him to accept Wieman's dismissal of trinitarianism as lacking empirical support — a safe gambit since no one ever suggested that the ultimate mystery of the Trinity could be demonstrated empirically. Thus while dissociating himself from Wieman's rejection of a personal God, King wavered on the underlying contention that personality can only arise from a society of interrelating individuals.

On this politically charged theological problem, King slid toward incoherence, apparently unaware of a critical literature his professors did not bother to assign to their students. Thus he sensibly insisted that the personality of God should be understood as absolute and not confused with human personality, but he showed no sense that the concept of the Trinity itself expressed interpersonal relations within the Godhead. If King had read the leading theologians of his native South, most notably James Henley Thornwell and Robert L. Dabney, he would have had to confront a defense of trinitarian doctrine that asserted a triune God who expressed interpersonality.

No amount of appeals to the superiority of African spirituality over the allegedly Hellenic and overly intellectualized elitism of "Euro-Christianity" can compensate for the deficiency. For the appeal does violence to another and more plausible claim — that African and Afro-American folk culture compel significant revisions in Christian theology itself. To defend that claim, which may indeed have merit, proponents cannot avoid the responsibility to demonstrate specifically how black folk culture compels rethinking of such fundamental problems as the relation of the Creation to the Incarnation, the Fall, the nature of sin, and the Atonement.

The implications of the course taken by King and his successors remain politically troubling, for they suggest a gap between the spirituality of black Christians and the theologians who speak in their name. As a political leader, King came on the scene at a decisive historical moment and proved equal to the tasks his people and, presumably, his God set for him. Even if his theology intrinsically left much to be desired and in some ways abstractly separated his views from the sensibility of his people, the attendant difficulties were as nothing in the context of the exigencies of the great social struggle on which he and they had embarked. His successors, in asserting their own version of a disembodied Socinianism, may not emerge as so fortunate.

Notwithstanding the warm approbation of King's professors, his critique of the doctrine of original sin was appallingly weak. "On moral grounds," he declared, "a person cannot be punished in the place of another." Following in the footsteps of the Abolitionist theologians during the slavery controversy, King wrote as if man tells God what is moral and what is sinful, instead of God telling man. But if so, in what could King ground his appeal to an absolute truth in ethics? That quibble aside, King, in the qualifying examination for the doctorate, insisted that guilt and punishment are not transferable from one person to another. "It seems much more logical," he concluded, "to find the origin of sin in man's free will. Sin originates when man misuses his freedom." The socialistic King seems not have noticed that, in discussing sin, he was sliding onto radical-individualist ground, implicitly rejecting the collective nature of sin as derived from Adam as the representative of humanity as a whole.

Here as elsewhere, King takes Arminian ground, but serious Arminians understand that they must separate two distinct parts of the Calvinist argument if they are to reply satisfactorily: the free will attributed to Adam during the probationary period in which God placed him, and the corruption of the will that rendered man "dead in sin" after the Fall. Apparently, King never heard of such doctrines as "Numerical Identity" or the "Federal Theology," which present powerful challenges to his argument. Let us restrict ourselves to the Federal Theology. King frequently cited Calvin's *Institutes*, which, arguably, contains an interpretation of Adam as the federal representative of a human race that collectively sinned through him. Then and now, any theology student ought to be acquainted with the elaboration, defense, and development of the Federal Theology by a long line of outstanding Calvinists. It should be enough to mention Charles Hodge, whose *Systematic Theology* long held pride of place in American Calvinist circles.

King did ponder the nature and ubiquity of sin, struggling bravely with its political implications. While still in his teens he caviled at liberal theology's rosy view of human nature and admired the neo-orthodox emphasis on man's ubiquitous sinfulness. He criticized the "strong tendency" in liberal Protestantism toward "a sentimental view of man" and rejected perfectionism and the political utopianism it encouraged. Thus in a paper on "Contemporary Continental Theology," he wrote that such optimism has been discredited by "the brutal logic of events"; that man appears to be "more of a sinner than liberals are willing to admit"; and that "many of the ills of the world are due to plain sin." He concluded: "The word sin must come back into our vocabulary." This paper, too, was heavily plagiarized, but, as in his other work, plagiarism or no, King was asserting deeply held views that remained with him throughout his life. And he was developing a language through which he could lay the foundation for an ultimate reconciliation with conservative Southern whites, which he knew to be essential to the long-run success of the black cause.

Problems nonetheless recurred. When King wrote of the "logic of events," rather than events, he suggested a theory of inherent sinfulness, but he had no discernible explanation of its origins. He approvingly referred to Reinhold Niebuhr's view that sin arises from man's refusal to admit his creatureliness and from his pretension to being more than he is. But Niebuhr accepted the doctrine of original sin, whereas King, as he himself noted, could offer no alternate explanation for an inherent sinfulness.

King did better with the political manifestations of sinfulness, taking an admirable stance toward burden and responsibility. Reviewing his people's responses to the terrible afflictions they have suffered, he espoused the doctrine, recently espoused eloquently by Nicholas Cooper-Lewter and Henry H.

Mitchell, that God only demands of us what we are capable of fulfilling — that He places upon us no burdens He has not given us the capacity to bear. Theologically, this formulation may be contested sharply, although it has proved well-nigh indispensable for pastoral work. In any case, the constructive political uses to which King put it remain striking. For he translated it into an impatient refusal to make "oppression" an excuse for avoiding personal responsibility for destructive actions and inactions.

THE PROBLEMATIC relation of King's theology to his politics surfaces in his doctrine of nonviolence. The defeat of legal segregation signaled the end of America's formal adherence to racist ideology, for, as Thurgood Marshall and his team of civil rights lawyers forcefully argued before the Supreme Court, the rationale for segregation implied the racial inferiority of blacks. The great struggle that followed the Court's historic decision of 1954 was, therefore, revolutionary, for it overthrew centuries-long constitutional, social, political, and institutional structures and practices. King, boldly challenging the leaders of the older civil rights movement, in effect turned to revolutionary measures, but, in accordance with his deepest religious beliefs as well as his political realism, he demanded that the necessary program, however revolutionary, eschew violence.

Two weeks after *Brown v. Board of Education*, King demonstrated the seriousness with which he considered nonviolence an expression of Christian faith rather than merely a political tactic. He devoted a sermon in Montgomery to a theme that he would return to again and again: "Loving Your Enemies." Indeed, from his student days onward he exhibited that seriousness in his critique of communism. King, despite a misreading of Marx as an economic determinist, saw much to praise in his theory of class power, but he worried much over the lack of a moral perspective in Marxism. He especially recoiled from the totalitarian tendency inherent in materialist philosophy and its implicit ethical relativism. In his student days, he flayed the atheistic dialectics of Marxism-Leninism, and in 1961 he identified "the greatest tragedy of communism" as its doctrine that the end justifies the means, which translates into a justification for "lying, deceit, or violence" in the service of "the classless society."

In espousing nonviolence in his "I Have a Dream" speech, King called for an imitation of Christ that would reconcile oppressed and oppressors — would lead "the sons of slaves and the sons of slaveholders to sit down together at the table of brotherhood." In effect, he invoked the Christian concept of forgiveness, which should not be confused with the sentimentality according to which "to understand is to forgive." King always stressed that Christians must seek forgiveness through confession and repentance, doing everything in their power to undo the damage they have done. Racial reconciliation therefore requires that whites do everything in their power to exorcise the legacy of slavery and racism.

But King was also speaking directly to blacks, admonishing them to eschew hatred, which, however "understandable," could only destroy their own souls. King, invoking nonviolence as Christian principle, was offering a therapy designed to prevent the oppressed from becoming the mirror image of the worst of their oppressors. He never wavered in his conviction that no just society could emerge from a mere reversal of roles — a theme well developed by Theophus H. Smith, *Conjuring Culture: Biblical Formations of Black America*. In speeches during the late 1950's and 60's, King hammered at the theme that the movement must seek reconciliation, not the humiliation of adversaries. Speaking at Lincoln University in Pennsylvania in 1961, he said:

"As I have said in so many instances, it is not enough to struggle for the new society. We must make sure that we make the psychological adjustment required to live in that new society. This is true of white people, and it is true of Negro people. Psychological adjustment will save white people from going into the new age with old vestiges of prejudice and attitudes of white supremacy. It will save the Negro from seeking to substitute one tyranny for another."

The principle and strategy of nonviolence proceeded in high tension with the resort to revolutionary measures, manifested in mass demonstrations against the law of the land and the juropolitical system itself. King was engaging in high-rolling and embarking on a dangerous course. Even Thurgood Marshall initially condemned him for his mobilization of young students to defy the law, sneering that the struggle for civil rights was a job for men, not children, and describing King as a "first-rate rabble-rouser."

However dangerous the course, King grasped its special promise, and he proved Marshall wrong. Digging deep into the religio-
political experience of his people, he appealed to the prophetic
tradition to invoke symbols that were likely to resonate among
the white Americans whose support the black cause desper-
ately needed. King grounded nonviolence in Scripture and
Christian ethics. The sincerity of his stern denunciations of
violence is clear enough, but his doctrine contains some painful political and ethical problems. No more than Thoreau,
Tolstoy, Gandhi, or the more recent figures who, especially
since the 1960's, have distinguished force from violence did
King squarely face the contradiction in his position. Gandhi
preached nonviolence as forcefully as any man, but large numbers of his followers repeatedly resorted to extreme violence.
Gandhi condemned them for violating his teachings, but when
followers repeatedly slip into violations we must ask whether the
teachings themselves do not carry the seeds of opposite doctrine.

Force generates counterforce. If people have a "right" to use
force against others and against the state, those under siege
have an equivalent "right" to defend themselves. And rights
or no, historical experience demonstrates that they usually will
defend themselves, invoking the unassailable principle that
self-preservation is the most firmly grounded of all rights. When
force meets counterforce, violence ensues. When, for example,
demonstrators exercise their presumed right to sit down and
block entrance to the office of a university president, the president may readily claim an equivalent right to walk into his
office. If he insists upon walking, he will have to step on those

who are sitting down. When his foot meets the body of a demonstrator, we have an act of violence. But whose violence? Those who sit down assume that the president must either surrender his office or accept responsibility for the consequences of his unwillingness to be intimidated.

I imply no equation of the moral positions of oppressors and oppressed. Politically, the presumably oppressed may have a strong case for their action, especially if, as is often the case, they have been denied effective and lawful means of redress. But that is only another way of saying that violence may some- 'times be justified. Responsibility inescapably rests with those who initiate the confrontation on grounds of principle, of ethical imperative, of Higher Law. The one thing they cannot do is play Pontius Pilate and wash their hands of responsibility for the probable consequences. And manifestly, King refused to play Pontius Pilate. To his credit, he preached that those who feel compelled by conscience to break the law must be pre- pared to suffer accordingly.

Still, the example of Tolstoy, whose religio-social views King admired, might have led him to reflect upon the anarchism to which they led. King, like Tolstoy, invoked the Sermon on the Mount, which he interpreted in accordance with his view that God gives us only such burdens as we can bear. King viewed Jesus as a God-conscious man who demonstrated how human beings could resist temptation through strict obedience to God's law. Jesus' sacrifice on the Cross for the redemption of human- ity was a supreme act of obedience. Since Jesus as God was impervious to sin, we might ask how could He have experienced temptation in a manner equivalent to that experienced by an ordinary man. Some of the explanations advanced by theologians are ingenious, but it remains doubtful that anyone has yet squared the circle.

Trinitarians surely must cavil at King's doctrine of burden and capacity, for if Jesus is viewed as Incarnation and as a Second Adam born without sin but simultaneously the Second Person of the Godhead, every effort at the Imitation of Christ must fall short of perfection. Men cannot, for example, be expected to turn the other cheek while wife and children are under assault. But then, could any man in this world live wholly in accordance with the words of Jesus? In an implicit rejection of King's formulation, Jaroslav Pelikan has tersely observed that Jesus demanded a perfection beyond human capacity. The very point of the Sermon on the Mount is to reassert and explicate the Old Testament Decalogue and thereby to remind us that we are all guilty of sin and that the heart of man is known only to God. The Sermon on the Mount reinforces our awareness of unworthiness and of dependence upon the grace of God for a redemption we have not earned.

The problem arises not from King's invocation of the Sermon on the Mount, but from an interpretation that leads inexorably to the transformation of Jesus into a mere moral teacher and to the secularization of ethics. With that implicit secularization goes a strong tendency, which a worried King tried to resist, toward the abstraction of evils from the nature of man and the attribution of them to social relations and institutions. It is a short step to the demonization of the supporters of those social relations and institutions which we may deem sinful.

King himself tirelessly preached that Christian ethics without Christian love generates self-righteous attacks on the sinners as readily as on the sin, if indeed not more so. In this matter, despite frequent accusations to the contrary, he practiced what he preached. He took second place to none in adhering to the Christian admonition to hate the sin but love the sinner. At issue here is not the sincerity of his moral stance but the contradiction between it and the logic of his religio-political theory. Those who, often while espousing nonviolence, assume responsibility for the initiation of physical confrontations may be more deeply moved by revulsion against injustice than are those who defend social order, but their claims to moral rectitude do not relieve them of the responsibility to have available a tenable alternate social order that promises to eradicate existing evils without creating worse ones.

King confronted the most perplexing problems of our age and led a heroic effort to solve them in a manner worthy of a civilized nation. He achieved as much as he did because he had the precious gift of an intellect and a will capable of bringing an effective politics out of considerable doctrinal incoherence. That gift manifests itself as political genius, and men who have it come along rarely.

The danger today is that we may replay a story that has recurred throughout history. All great leaders are deeply flawed, but their greatness arises from their ability to manifest their best and rein in their worst at those very moments when the world must depend upon their statesmanship. Unfortunately, even talented and well-meaning successors are rarely themselves great men. More often than not, they build as readily on the errors of their predecessors as on their statesmanship. Those who would carry forward King's legacy cannot expect to achieve anything at all if they do not begin with a thorough critique of his thought in relation to his action, distinguishing carefully between those actions which flowed from his nobility, insight, and wisdom and those which flowed from his doctrinal confusions and personal weaknesses.

Martin Luther King, Jr., should be judged, as we should all expect to be judged — on the balance of his life's work. With faith, wisdom, courage, and extraordinary political skill he led a social and political revolution in American race relations and thereby earned the admiration and gratitude of the world. Yes, King had a full quotient of faults, some of them grievous, for, like the rest of us, he was a man. But, unlike the rest of us, he was a great man.

Chapter Eight

DEATH THREATS, LIES, AND THE
FUTURE OF AMERICAN CULTURE

Three death threats, one left hook to the jaw, 40 rejections from 40 publishers in 40 months, and a sold-out first edition. This rather well describes the varied response to this book. Regarding the 40 publishers, their rejections were entertaining, as well as enlightening. Three of them said a book critical of any aspect of Martin Luther King, Jr.'s life or work would be in "bad taste," because "King isn't around to defend himself." When I replied that this absurd standard would mean the end of historical studies and of scholarship in general — that this standard has not hindered the rise of our new national pastime, defaming Thomas Jefferson — I not only received no responses but in one case even got my letter back stamped, "Return to Sender" — the publisher had not even opened it. A handful of them said, "Great book, we're definitely interested, now just give equal time to the other side of the story." By "equal time" they meant a nonjudgmental discussion of the "voice merging" bilge. According to this standard, no writer could praise free trade without also praising tariffs and protectionism.

But killing debate and stifling discussion were not these publishers' true objectives. It was only killing *this* debate, suppressing *this* discussion — and smothering any other hint of free thinking that might disturb the verbal industries and their manufacturing of public truth — that really concerns them. The "reader's recommendation" of one publisher gave away the game: "I recommend against publishing this book, because such honesty and truth-telling could only be destructive." The end of culture is closer than we think.

Other publishers wrote off this book as a right-wing screed, even though my most vocal critics have issued from the right: meaning neoconservatives, who tolerate no criticism of King, no matter how tempered or just, because King is their new-found champion of conservatism; and white racists, who expected this book to be a down-and-dirty dose of King-bashing and were disappointed. In fact, the leading "conservative" academic publisher today rejected this book because I failed to sing the virtues of the civil rights movement. When I replied that the book's subject was plagiarism and cultural standards and not the civil rights movement, whatever the latter's virtues, this publisher replied, "It doesn't matter what your purpose is."

Concerning the death threats, only one of them was memorable, and only memorable for its tackiness: it was left on my answering machine on the morning of my wedding. Regarding the left hook to my jaw, thrown by an inebriated critic who recognized me from an interview then running on the barroom TV — it missed.

Death threats against American writers who refuse to toe the politically correct line are not as uncommon as one might think. Historian David Hackett Fischer of Brandeis University received death threats in the wake of his *Albion's Seed*, published in 1989. As he explained in "Telling Stories in the New Age," in the March 1997 issue of *Chronicles*, "a book that argued for the importance of having been English was not thought to be politically correct. A book that gave much attention to themes of continuity from past to present was not thought to be historically correct. A book that centered on the determinant power of individual choice was not thought to be ontologically correct." And so the death threats began, most of them postmarked from university towns, and all of them crudely lettered. The plodding prose of the letters should have tipped off the FBI and the Postmaster General that the threats came from members of the academic community, but later evidence left no room for doubt: one of the death threats came with footnotes.

No more evidence is needed; the verdict is in: nothing is more intolerant of a diversity of opinion than a "liberal" society touting the virtues of tolerance and diversity.

"INTOLERANT" MAY be the best way to describe the recent developments in the King plagiarism story, and the actions in particular of the King estate. It is difficult to overstate just how severely the King family's missteps, profiteering, and general uncooperativeness have damaged King's legacy in the black community. The King family's surprising announcement that they believed James Earl Ray to have been innocent of the murder of MLK — as many commentators countered, Ray may not have pulled the trigger, but he certainly was guilty of *something* — is just one of the many decisions that have raised eyebrows and invited censure.

When King's son Dexter became president of the Martin Luther King Jr. Center for Nonviolent Social Change in Atlanta for a second time in 1994 — Dexter, a Morehouse College dropout and former rap music producer, had quit after serving only four months as president in 1989 — he immediately consolidated control over his family's social programs and financial affairs. According to Kevin Sack of the *New York Times* ("A Different Dream, Sheen of the King Legacy Dims On New, More Profitable Path," August 19, 1997), Dexter's overriding concern was how to transform the King legacy into a financial empire and a windfall in particular for the King family. Dexter first overhauled the board of directors of the King Center so that family members held a majority of the seats and then "orchestrated the premature shutdown of the Martin Luther King Jr. Federal Holiday Commission . . . because he saw it as a fundraising competitor of the center." The King family next battled the National Park Service's revitalization plan of King's Auburn Avenue neighborhood. The family reportedly pulled out all the stops, especially against the Park Service's plan to build a visitors center and museum directly across the street from the King Center. They first demanded that the Park Service triple its annual half-million dollar payment to the King Center (the Center reportedly received half of its $4.2 million budget from government grants in 1996). They then contacted Interior Secretary Bruce Babbitt in an effort to kill the Park Service's plans altogether. And when this too failed, the King family cried "racism." "The same evil forces that killed Martin Luther King, Jr., are now trying to destroy his family," said Mrs. King. Dexter compared the Park Service's "encroachment and annexation" in the King Center's neighborhood to the federal government's genocidal policies toward Native Americans.

And why did the King family so vehemently object to plans which the family, by many accounts, had initially supported? It seems Dexter now wanted the site of the Park Service's facilities for a money-making venture. According to Ken Ringle of the *Washington Post* ("Whose Dream Is It Now?" January 16, 1995), Dexter planned to build a $60 million high-tech Martin Luther King Jr. Time Machine and Interactive Museum; it would be a Disneyland-style facility that even marketed King trinkets and figurines, not unlike the image marketing of Elvis at Graceland and of

Malcolm X in the recent years. Cynthia Tucker of the staunchly liberal *Atlanta Journal/Constitution* mocked the idea as "a sort of I have a Dreamland." John Lewis, U.S. Representative (D-GA) and former King ally during the civil rights movement, was equally appalled. "Dr. King's legacy shouldn't be up for sale like soap," he told the *Wall Street Journal.*

Having lost the battle, Mrs. King then focused attention on the Park Service itself, arguing "a federal agency is poorly qualified to interpret the 'people's' history. That responsibility is better left to the people who lived it." Mrs. King has a point, and many would agree that the federal government should not be in the business of marketing heroes to the American people. But her insinuation that the revitalization plan was somehow a white scheme being shoved down the throat of the black community outraged Atlanta. The entire community — both white and black, and especially the poor black residents of the Auburn Avenue neighborhood — had fought long and hard to implement and fund this revitalization plan, to which Congress allocated $11.8 million in 1993. Moreover, the Park Service superintendent in charge of the King facilities is a middle-aged black man who was born and raised in the segregated town of Valdosta, Georgia, sinking the contention that this plan is run by people estranged from the black community's history and plight.

Criticism of the King family came fast and furiously. "It's like a monarchy," said Mtamanika Youngblood, executive director of the Historic District Development Corp., to journalist Eric Harrison ("Rev. King's Family Challenges Park Service Project," *Washington Post*, December 26, 1994). "She's [Coretta King] a queen, and Dexter is a prince." Said a black businessman in Atlanta to Ken Ringle of the *Post*: "She [Coretta King] lobbied effectively for the King holiday, and she'll fly anywhere to get her picture taken with Nelson Mandela. But when thousands of our kids are killing each other in the streets, she wants the King Center . . . to hold meaningless awards and fashion shows during King week . . . to raise money so they can hold more awards dinners and fashion shows next year." Veteran civil rights leader Julian Bond, in the *New York Times*: "If they [the King family] are the repository of King's legacy, I don't see much being done to spread the message of his life and work." Said another Atlanta businessman: the King family has "alienated thousands of people who revere Martin's memory and would otherwise have walked through fire with them to help them make his dream a reality." Ringle agreed, saying "despite a presence in the neighborhood for nearly 30 years, the Kings have shown no such concern for the poor and the powerless, for whom King himself once labored. 'They forgot what he was about,' said Frankie Ross, an elderly Auburn Avenue resident. 'The Park Service is the one these days that makes everyone remember.'"

This harsh criticism of the King family might be shocking to the general reader, for the mainstream, predominantly white corporate media have generally refused to discuss this tension in the black community over control of the King legacy. "What is finally surfacing," concludes Ringle, "is a longtime tendency of the King family — like the families of many other famous people the world over — to live off King's legacy rather than advance it. It is a tendency that's been wryly noted for years here [in Atlanta] and in the wider civil rights community, but rarely mentioned publicly out of respect for King's memory." In other words, in the name of sensitivity and the "higher good" — the same catchall justification for suppressing the King plagiarism story — the white corporate media have decided not to cover issues and debates they deem not in the best interest of the black community. Jesse Jackson is right: racism and discrimination are alive and well in America.

But with regard to King's writings, it is Dexter King's deal with Phillip Jones of Intellectual Properties Management (IPM) and Time-Warner that most concerns the academic community, liberal social activists, and long-time friends and followers of King. Under Jones's tutelage, the King estate has reportedly reached financial terms with filmmaker Oliver Stone to make a movie about King, agreed to an entertainment show hosted by Dick Clark each January to commemorate the King holiday, and according to Sack of the *New York Times*, has even negotiated with a Disney subsidiary on a one-hour animated special "about some kids who go back in time and meet a young Martin," which according to Dexter King "would be shown each year like 'Peanuts Christmas.'" But it is the lucrative deal with Time-Warner, which was announced in January 1997, that has raised the ire of writers and scholars. According to this plan, Time-Warner will produce and market new books of King's writings, memoirs by family members, recordings and CD-ROM's of King's speeches, and a King-related Internet site; the deal will reportedly net the King estate $30-$50 million within five years.

At the heart of the deal is an aggressive enforcement of the hundreds of copyrights that King placed on "his" writings and on his most famous speeches in particular. Most disturbing, especially to the black community, has been the King family's aggressive profiteering toward those wanting to praise King by quoting the "I Have a Dream" speech. When *USA Today* quoted the speech in praise of King in 1993, the King estate sued; the newspaper had to pay a $1,700 licensing fee plus legal costs. When CBS simply reran its original news footage of King giving the "I Have a Dream" speech in Washington in 1963 as part of its five-part video documentary called "The 20th Century With Mike Wallace," the King estate also sued.

But it is not just corporate giants who have been hassled and hindered in their attempt to celebrate the King legacy. When a newspaper editor in Lexington, Kentucky, wanted to honor King by printing one of his speeches from 1965, IPM made him jump through hoops to gain permission. The editor's ordeal, according to David Garrow's account of it in the *Washington Post* ("Are They Stifling the Work of Martin Luther King, Jr.?" January 28, 1997), was "long and frustrating." "Despite an express-delivery letter and phone calls, he could not get a timely answer; only at the last minute did his newspaper receive approval to reprint the speech."

This oppugnancy is apparently par for the course. As Kevin Sack noted in the *Times*, "The interview with [Dexter] King for this article, first requested on April 7, was granted on Aug. 1, and only after lengthy negotiation. Repeated requests for interviews with Mrs. King and her other children were declined." Ken Ringle of the *Post* had the same experience: "For three days repeated phone calls to the five listed numbers for the King Center rang unanswered, though later visits found the center amply staffed. Other journalists at the center warned that King family members 'do everything through spokespeople who never call back.' When a king Center spokeswoman, Zee Bradford, finally appeared, . . . she took [my] business card and never called back."

Major corporate sponsors of the King estate's programs have received the same treatment. Ringle notes that Coca-Cola, British Petroleum, and Ford Motor Company are among the major corporations that have withdrawn their support from the King estate out of frustration and dissatisfaction. An IBM executive told the *Washington Post*, "We were ready to commit quite a fair amount of money with them. But we kept running up against what seemed to be their complete inability to operate by even the most minimal standards of a business. . . . We developed this one interactive display and tried to have them put it out where visitors could see it, but instead they insisted on keeping it in a back room where they could play with it." Finally, "somebody stole part of one machine and we just decided to hell with it and gave up. It was very disheartening."

But it is not just this lack of cooperation that bothers writers, journalists, scholars, and editors: once permission is granted to reprint King's work, the fees charged by the King estate are also often excessive. Richard Lischer, a professor of divinity at Duke University, told the *New York Times* that his book *The Preacher King* (1995) was delayed for a whole year while "the [King] estate's literary agent reviewed the manuscript for copyright violations." Moreover, "I thought their demands for payment for quotations in a serious study of King were excessive." So reportedly were the fees charged Julian Bond for reprinting four documents in his 824-page textbook on civil rights. "The book costs 65 bucks, and the publisher told me those documents put the price up 10 or 15 dollars a book. . . . I was prepared to pay something. It just seemed to me an unreasonable charge." Philip Jones of IPM agreed, saying the fees charged Bond, in a deal struck before the King family had hired IPM, were indeed exorbitant. Taylor Branch, a Pulitzer Prize-winning biographer of King, was even more candid. As he reportedly told the *Daily Report* of Fulton County, Georgia, scholarship "would grind to a halt" if the King family's approach to intellectual property rights became widely accepted.

Mr. Branch is right: by delaying publishing projects with excessive red tape, or by derailing them altogether with exorbitant fees, the King estate can in effect stymie scholarship and censor history by controlling who receives permission to comment on King and his work. This danger was not lost on David Garrow, a frequent critic of the King family. As he wrote in "Are They Stifling the Work of Martin Luther King, Jr.?":

How will new students of King's life, especially young people, react to the meaning of a man whose year-2000 image may be heavily colorized — or perhaps bleached — by Time-Warner's corporate image specialists? . . . Consider the possibility of a scholar whose analyses of King — or anything else — anger or offend the King estate. . . . Could permission to quote from King's materials be withheld, or the price made high enough to alone block publication?

As a case in point, Garrow highlights the ostensible about-face of Taylor Branch, who after meeting with Dexter King then "declined to expand" on his previous public criticisms of the King estate. "Branch may or may not have changed his views [on the King estate]," writes Garrow, "but the leverage that IPM's stance gives the King estate over writers who specialize in King could well inhibit them from speaking out fully and frankly about their concerns regarding the King family, the King Center and the King estate."

The Reverend Joseph E. Lowery of the Southern Christian Leadership Conference has indeed spoken frankly. Though he did not object to the Time-Warner deal in principle, he expressed dismay that the King family has shown no interest in sharing their forthcoming windfall. After all, he told the New York Times, King's words were often preserved on "tapes made by S.C.L.C. staff and S.C.L.C. equipment."

According to Sack, Dexter King discounts the criticisms of his family by veteran civil rights leaders as "the growling of old lions," and the criticisms by Garrow as part of a vendetta against his family. (Dexter claims Garrow is mad over not being selected to edit King's papers, a charge Garrow denies.) But Garrow's concern about scholarly and nonscholarly access to King's writings have been expressed by others, long before the deal with IPM and Time-Warner. The National Endowment for the Humanities, which funds the King Papers Project and the King Center archives, reportedly explained in writing to Coretta King as far back as 1977 that the endowment could not support "collections to which scholarly access is restricted to any significant degree or whose physical availability is limited." According to Louise Cook, a King Center archivist quoted in the New York Times, "Mrs. King had failed to live up to pledges made to the endowment in the 1970's and 1980's that she would move documents from her house to the center."

What is overlooked in all of this is the irony: the King estate now enforces copyrights and demands royalties on work which King often stole in the first place. In a just world, the royalties would go to estates of Jack Boozer, Archibald Carey, Paul Tillich, and to the scores of other writers, ministers, scholars, and social activists whose work fell prey to King's "voice merging."

But the King family's blunders and blustering are not alone responsible for King's troubled legacy. For if by "King's legacy" one means a vision of racial harmony and cultural inclusiveness, of a society based not on race and special treatment but on character, merit, and mutual respect — which is the common view of the King legacy as generated by white leaders and the national media, which, according to Jeff Cohen and Norman Solomon (Media Beat, January 4, 1995), deliberately do not air King's speeches from 1966 to 1968, the radical ones which excited black activists but horrified white liberals, because they are detrimental to the "correct" King legacy — then it is all the dubious things done today in King's name that hinder this "dream" from becoming a reality. When Jesse Jackson celebrates the King holiday by leading students in the chant,

"Hey, hey, ho, ho, Western culture's got to go!" — as he did at Stanford University in 1987; when one of our finer colleges invites an Afrocentrist to instruct its students in historical myths and anti-Western vitriol as part of the school's annual Martin Luther King, Jr., Memorial Lecture, and then upbraids any faculty members who object, as Wellesley College did in 1993; when black "leaders" say King's words are for "authentic blacks" only, that neither black Republicans ("Uncle Toms") nor white liberals opposed to discrimination, including reverse discrimination, have the "right" to quote King's "I Have a Dream" speech; when Boston University's Martin Luther King, Jr., Professor of Social Ethics embarrasses himself, his chair, and his university by announcing there is no "blatancy" in King's plagiarisms, that "there is no obvious indication in [King's] dissertation that he inappropriately utilized material" — they breed divisiveness, not unity, and do a disservice not only to scholarship, to the country, and to this particular view of King's legacy but to minority youth in desperate need of real history and heroes whose virtues and vices they can study and learn from.

"It really is time to move past all this," concludes William Murchison of the *Dallas Morning News* ("Sensibility on Martin Luther King," January 11, 1995). "The Kennedys and King are '60s icons who got shot in turbulent times now mercifully behind us. This hardly qualifies them for the sainthood they have since received." D.C. Representative Eleanor Holmes Norton is even franker. When William Bennett agreed in a debate with her that people should be judged by the "content of their character" and not the "color of their skin," she angrily retorted, "Stop quoting dead saints!"

Murchison has a point: we do need to temper our often maudlin and romanticized picture of the 1960's with some historical perspective and sensibility, and this certainly has occurred in recent years with regards to the amphetamine-addicted, skirt-chasing Golden Boy of Camelot. On the other hand, Martin Luther King, Jr., was (and is) a mighty man to millions of Americans, white and black, who will never "stop quoting him" and who will never simply view him as a "60's icon." He is much more than this, and always will be. The question is: How much more? And can Americans and American scholars even debate such a question when an all-encompassing shroud protects this courageous but controversial and obviously flawed man from even the most cursory of scrutiny?

A revisionist picture of King has been emerging, but not without great risk to those trying to stem the mythologizing of the man. Not even King's dearest friend and closest confidant, Ralph Abernathy, could discuss King's life with impunity. When he discussed King's final days and extramartial affairs in And the Walls Came Tumbling Down (1989) — when he tried, in his words, "to portray Martin as a believable human being" — the mainstream media and the civil rights establishment would have none of it. They cried "foul," and according to the smear campaign that followed, Abernathy was "vindictive," "jealous," and a "traitor" to his people, to the "movement," and to his martyred friend; others dismissed his comments as the ramblings of a dying and doddery old fool.

But as Abernathy understood, the problem is clearly that King has left the realm of the human: he is no longer a man to be understood but a deity to be worshipped, revered, and glorified — only worshipped, revered, and glorified. And as the ancients wondered, how can mere mortals question a god?

Manning Marable, a professor of history and the director of the Institute for Research in African-American Studies at Columbia University, admits in Speaking Truth to Power: Essays on Race, Resistance, and Radicalism (1996) that "our images of Malcom [X] and Martin [Luther King, Jr.]

are drawn less by what they actually accomplished as individual political actors . . . than by the weight of what we collectively are told about them within contemporary culture." King moves

> from the role of creative and insightful political leader to the semi-frozen state of becoming a cultural icon, with coldly chiseled features. . . . The great danger with this form of lionization is that, regardless of well-meaning motivations, it is destructive and dangerous, particularly for the oppressed. The real value of historical greatness is not the simple-minded praising of figures like King and Malcolm X. . . . Both of these men were profoundly human. They made errors, mistakes, misjudgments of all kinds.

Marable's comments speak a truth which many do not want to hear. Potted histories and hagiographies packed with lies and listings of wrongs and oppressions, both real and imagined, only ensure the despair of minorities today; they fill them with false hope, consume them with hate, normalize their failures, and fuel racial discord. Professional race-baiters and their self-hating allies call this "empowerment," "consciousness-raising," and social progress, but we know where such pish-posh eventually leads. Lies were the pillar of the Soviets' state, and lies bred the chaos and disillusionment that sealed their fate. Though the "city upon a hill" is loath to admit it, there are some truths not even America can afford to ignore.

NOTES AND REFERENCES

1. Thomas Sowell, *Civil Rights: Rhetoric or Reality?* (New York: William Morrow and Company, Inc., 1984), 7.

2. The first edition of this book was published as *The Martin Luther King, Jr., Plagiarism Story* by The Rockford Institute in Rockford, Illinois, in 1994. Portions of this chapter appeared in "Plagiarism, Culture, and the Future of the Academy," *Humanitas* (Volume VI, No. 2, 1993); "All Such Filthy Cheats," *Chronicles: A Magazine of American Culture*, September 1994; "Peddlers of Virtue," *Chronicles*, May 1995; and in the introduction to the first edition of this book.

3. See Charles J. Sykes' *ProfScam: Professors and the Demise of Higher Education* (Washington, D.C.: Regnery Gateway, 1988); Roger Kimball's *Tenured Radicals: How Politics Has Corrupted Higher Education* (New York: Harper & Row, 1990); Arthur Schlesinger, Jr.'s *The Disuniting of America: Reflections on a Multicultural Society* (New York: W.W. Norton, 1991); James Davison Hunter's *Culture Wars: The Struggle to Define America* (New York: BasicBooks, 1991); Richard Bernstein's *Dictatorship of Virtue: Multiculturalism and the Battle for America's Future* (New York: Alfred A. Knopf, 1994); Christopher Lasch's *The Revolt of the Elites and the Betrayal of Democracy* (New York: W.W. Norton, 1995);

and Mary Lefkowitz's *Not Out of Africa: How Afrocentricism Became an Excuse to Teach Myth as History* (New York, BasicBooks, 1996).

4. From a 1993 interview of Bernard Violet by Pierre Prier of *The European*.

5. Peter Shaw, "Plagiary," *American Scholar* (Summer 1982), 325-337.

6. Thomas Mallon, *Stolen Words: Forays into the Origins and Ravages of Plagiarism* (New York: Ticknor and Fields, 1989).

7. Robert K. Massie, "Safire and Me," *Nation* (February 14, 1994), 184-185.

8. Mallon, *Stolen Words*, 127-130; Trudy Lieberman, "Plagiarize, Plagiarize, Plagiarize," *Columbia Journalism Review* (July/August 1995), 21-25; Bruce Handy, "Steven Stealberg?" *Time* (November 24, 1997), 99; Margarett Loke, "Writer Who Cried Plagiarism Used Passages From Another," *New York Times* (December 19, 1997), A1.

9. Howard Kurtz, "Media Notes: Post Book Review Gets Unwelcome 2nd Printing," *Washington Post* (August 12, 1996), D1; Kurtz, "Media Notes: British Tabloid Alleges An Undiplomatic Affair," *Washington Post* (December 10, 1996), E1.

10. Christopher Hitchens, "Steal This Article," *Vanity Fair* (May 1996), 58-63; Jay Stowe, "Off the Record," *New York Observer* (May 27, 1996), 6.

11. For information on these various plagiarism controversies, see Shaw's "Plagiary" and Mallon's *Stolen Words*, as well as K. R. St. Onge, *The Melancholy Anatomy of Plagiarism* (Lanham, Maryland: University Press of America, 1988); Tom Fitzpatrick, "That's Spelled P-L-A-G-I-A-R-I-S-M," *Phoenix New Times*, September 1-7, 1993; Andrei Navrozov, "The Age of Plagiarism," *Times Magazine* of London, October 2, 1993;

Ron Grossman, "Silencing the Whistle: Plagiarism Cops Lose Their License to Embarrass," *Chicago Tribune*, May 10, 1993; Paul Gray, "The Purloined Letters," *Time*, April 26, 1993; Peter Shaw, "The Fatal Pattern of Plagiary," *Illinois Issues*, August/September 1991; John Meroney, "Maya Angelou's Inaugural Poem: Plagiarized or Inspired?" *Chronicles*, December 1993; Richard Johnson, "The Echo in Angelou's Poetry," *New York Post*, November 24, 1993; Martin Walker, "Angelou's Poetic Source Queried," *Manchester Guardian*, November 25, 1993; Norton F. Tennille, "A Rock, A River, A Tree / A Poetic Controversy," *Harper's*, March 1994; "Was He Really Bruno Borrowheim?" *Newsweek*, February 18, 1991; Richard Pollak, *The Creation of Dr. B: A Biography of Bruno Bettelheim* (New York: Simon & Schuster, 1997); Florence King, "Author, Author!" *American Enterprise*, November/December 1995; Howard Kurtz, "British Tabloid Alleges An Undiplomatic Affair," *Washington Post*, December 10, 1996; David Streitfeld, "Deepak Chopra, Meet Methuselah," *Washington Post*, July 21, 1995; Barry Baldwin, "Kadare's Concert: Some False Notes," *Friends of Albania*, Winter 1995; James R. Kincaid, "Purloined Letters: Are We Too Quick to Denounce Plagiarism?" *The New Yorker*, January 20, 1997; Philip Nobile, "Uncovering *Roots*," *Village Voice*, February 23, 1993; and Calvin Reid, "Fact or Fiction? Hoax Charges Still Dog 'Roots' 20 Years On," *Publishers Weekly*, October 6, 1997.

12. Kincaid, "Purloined Letters," 96-97.

13. Leonard B. Meyer, from his chapter "Forgery and the Anthropology of Art" in *Music, the Arts, and Ideas* (Chicago: University of Chicago Press, 1967) as reprinted in Denis Dutton's *The Forger's Art: Forgery and the Philosophy of Art* (Berkeley: University of California Press, 1983), 87.

14. Samuel Johnson, *The Rambler*, No. 143, July 30, 1751.

15. Dante, *The Inferno*, Canto XI, translated by John Ciardi (New York: Mentor, 1982), 104.

16. Mallon, *Stolen Words*, xiii-xiv.

17. Kincaid, "Purloined Letters," 97.

18. David Streitfeld, "Citing Plagiarism, Publisher Drops Book," *Washington Post* (April 19, 1994), D9.

19. Streitfeld, "Stolen Kisses!" *Washington Post*, (July 30, 1997), C1. See also Julia Duin, "'Victims' Hide Behind the Ethic of Excuses: Romance Writer Joins the Club," *Washington Times*, August 5, 1997.

20. The two texts are entitled: "Guide to the New GATT Agreement" by Joe Cobb and "A Report to the President, the Congress, and the United States Trade Representative Concerning the Uruguay Round of Negotiations on the General Agreement on Tariffs and Trade." See also Paul Gigot, *Wall Street Journal*, May 5, 1994, and "Heritage Economist Duplicates USTR Text," Ludwig von Mises Institute Report, January 1994.

21. The two texts are entitled: "NAFTA's Green Accords: Sound and Fury Signifying Little" (*Cato Policy Analysis* No. 198) and "The NAFTA Environmental Agreements" by Winthrop, Stimson, Putnam and Roberts of Washington D.C. See also "Cato Institute Scholar Copies Environmental Paper on NAFTA," Ludwig von Mises Institute Report, May 1995.

22. Al Kamen, "Sharing a Quote Among Conservatives," *Washington Post* (January 27, 1995), A23.

23. *Ibid.*

24. "The Book on Mr. Bennett's Virtue," *The New Yorker* (February 13, 1995), 33-34.

25. *Ibid.*, 34.

26. Stephen Nissenbaum, "The Plagiarists in Academe Must Face Formal Sanctions," *Chronicle of Higher Education* (March 28, 1990), A52.

27. Howard Goodman, "A Plagiaristic Footnote to History," *Philadelphia Inquirer* (April 28, 1994), A1; see also John O' Leary's "Plagiarism Student Named," London *Times*, October 13, 1994, and Ben Preston's "Oxford Plagiarist Loses Degree as Third Case Emerges," London *Times*, October 14, 1994.

28. C.P. Snow, *The Affair* (New York: Charles Scribner's Sons, 1960), 123.

29. Fox Butterfield, "For a Dean at Boston U., a Question of Plagiarism," *New York Times* (July 3, 1991), A14; David Nyhan, "When the Words Sound Too Familiar," *Boston Globe* (July 14, 1991), 73.

30. Patrick Buchanan, "America Must Tear Down the Icons of Liberalism," *Washington Times* (October, 16, 1991), F1.

31. See Hilary Groutage and Peggy Fletcher Stack, "BYU Leader Sorry for Speech's 'Ambiguity,'" *Salt Lake Tribune*, August 27, 1996, and Sharon M. Haddock, "Y. Leader Again Defends Himself," August 27, 1996.

32. Grossman, "Silencing the Whistle," *Chicago Tribune*, Tempo Section, 1. For other discussions of scientific fraud, see Judy Sarasohn, *Science on Trial: The Whistle-Blower, the Accused, and the Nobel Laureate* (New York: St. Martin's Press, 1993); Barbara Mishkin, "The Needless Agony and Expense of Conflict Among Scientists," *Chronicle of Higher Edu-*

cation, February 23, 1994; Rick Weiss, "Geneticist Accused of Fraud In Two Major Laboratories," *Washington Post*, October 30, 1996; Rick Weiss, "After Misconduct Probes, Some Scientists Are Fighting Back in Court," *Washington Post*, November 29, 1996.

33. Li Xiguang and Xiong Lei, "Chinese Researchers Debate Rash of Plagiarism Cases," *Science* (October 18, 1996), 337-338; Morton Hunt, "Did the Penalty Fit the Crime?" *New York Times Magazine*, (May 14, 1989), 69.

34. Xiguang and Lei, "Chinese Researchers," 337.

35. David Swinbanks, "Survey Battle Leads to Plagiarism Verdict," *Nature* (December 23/30, 1993), 715.

36. Nathaniel J. Pallone and James J. Hennessy, *Fraud and Fallible Judgment: Varieties of Deception in the Social and Behavioral Sciences* (New Brunswick: Transaction Publishers, 1995), 10. See also Gary Taubes, "Plagiarism Suit Wins; Experts Hope It Won't Set a Trend," *Science* (May 26, 1995), 1125.

37. Marcel C. LaFollette, *Stealing into Print: Fraud, Plagiarism, and Misconduct in Scientific Publishing* (Berkeley: University of California Press, 1992), 48-49. See also Robert Bell's *Impure Science: Fraud, Compromise, and Political Influence in Scientific Research* (New York: John Wiley & Sons, Inc., 1992).

38. Rex Stout, *Plot It Yourself* (New York: The Viking Press, 1959), 164.

39. *"Plagiat: Une Romanciere Tres Inspiree,"* *Le Point* (January 15, 1997), 32-33.

40. Quoted in Shaw, "Plagiary," 325.

41. Neal Bowers, *Words for the Taking: The Hunt for a Plagiarist* (New York: W.W. Norton & Company, 1997), 16.

42. Garry Wills, *Certain Trumpets: The Call of Leaders* (New York: Simon & Schuster, 1994), 219.

43. Jack Boozer learned about King's plagiarism in 1988, a full two years before the King Papers editors reluctantly released the evidence to the public. According to his wife, Boozer was disturbed by the plagiarism but "honored that he could have been of some help to Martin Luther." See "Widow Says Writer Didn't Care That King Copied," *New York Times* (November 11, 1990), A28.

44. Frank Kermode, "Profiles in Leadership," *New York Times Book Review* (April 24, 1994), 14.

45. Gossman, "Silencing the Whistle," Tempo Section, 1.

46. Charles Babington, "Embargoed," *New Republic* (January 28, 1991), 9-11.

47. For more information on John Reed's role in this case, and in particular on how his ties to the National Endowment for the Humanities, which also funds the Kings Papers Project, affected his decision to suppress his article, see Chris Raymond, "Discovery of Early Plagiarism by Martin Luther King Raises Troubling Questions for Scholars and Admirers," *Chronicle of Higher Education* (November 21, 1990), 1.

48. George A. Kennedy, *Classical Rhetoric and Its Christian and Secular Tradition from Ancient to Modern Times* (Chapel Hill: University of North Carolina, 1980), 28-29.

49. *The Suasoriae of Seneca the Elder*, iii, 7. Quoted in Harold Ogden White,

Plagiarism and Imitation During the English Renaissance: A Study in Critical Distinctions (Cambridge: Harvard University Press, 1935), 5-6.

50. Gilbert Highet, *The Classical Tradition: Greek and Latin Influences on Western Literature* (New York: Oxford University Press, 1949), 203.

51. From a November 24, 1882, letter to Mrs. S.E. Dawson. See Sir Edward Cook, *More Literary Recreations* (London: The Macmillan Company, 1919), 177-184 and Alexander Lindey, *Plagiarism and Originality* (New York: Harper & Brothers Publishers, 1952), 52-53.

52. Mallon, *Stolen Words*, 5.

53. Shaw, "Plagiary," 334.

54. *Ibid.*, 335.

55. "Report of the Boston University Committee to Investigate Charges of Plagiarism in the Ph.D. Dissertation of Martin Luther King, Jr." (September 1991), 2-4.

56. Shaw, "Plagiary," 335.

57. Keith D. Miller, *Voice of Deliverance: The Language of Martin Luther King, Jr. and Its Sources* (New York: The Free Press, 1992).

58. Eugene D. Genovese, "Pilgrim's Progress," *New Republic* (May 11, 1992), 35.

59. Genovese, from the foreword to this book and from "Publishing Matters II," *Common Knowledge* (Spring 1995), 98.

60. "Report of the Boston University Committee," Appendix D.

61. Mallon, *Stolen Words*, 24.

62. Miller, "Redefining Plagiarism: Martin Luther King's Use of an Oral Tradition," *Chronicle of Higher Education* (January 20, 1993), A60.

63. *Ibid.*

64. *Ibid.*

65. Ken Lebensold, "Plagiarism, Copyright, and Ownership of Ideas," *Chronicle of Higher Education* (February 24, 1993), B4.

66. Clayborne Carson, "Documenting Martin Luther King's Importance — and His Flaws," *Chronicle of Higher Education* (January 16, 1991), A52.

67. See in particular Book X of Quintilian's *Institutio Oratoria*.

68. Miller, *Voice of Deliverance*, 195.

69. Richard Lischer, *The Preacher King: Martin Luther King Jr. and The Word That Moved America* (New York: Oxford University Press, 1995), 114.

70. James Boswell, *The Life of Samuel Johnson*, letter dated August 30, 1780.

71. David J. Garrow, *Bearing the Cross: Martin Luther King, Jr., and the Southern Leadership Crisis* (New York: Morrow, 1986), 544; Georgia Davis Powers, *I Shared the Dream: The Pride, Passion and Politics of the First Black Woman Senator From Kentucky* (Far Hills, New Jersey: New Horizon Press, 1995), 158.

72. Walter Scott, "Personality Parade," *Parade* (August, 7, 1994), 2.

73. Miller, "Redefining Plagiarism," A60.

74. See David Streitfeld, "Publisher Drops Novel Over Pilfered Plot," *Washington Post* (February 17, 1994), A1; David Leavitt, "Did I Pla-

giarize His Life?" *New York Times Magazine* (April 3, 1994), 36-37; and Stephen Spender, "My Life Is Mine; It Is Not David Leavitt's," *New York Times Book Review* (September 4, 1994), 10-12.

75. Leavitt, "Did I Plagiarize His Life?", 37.
76. Miller, "Redefining Plagiarism," A60.
77. Anthony Grafton, *Forgers and Critics: Creativity and Duplicity in Western Scholarship* (Princeton: Princeton University Press, 1990), 127.
78. Bernstein, *Dictatorship of Virtue*, 231.
79. William Shakespeare, *Loves's Labour's Lost*, act 5, scene 2; *King Lear*, act 1, scene 2.

INDEX

Abernathy, Ralph, 83, 87, 101,143, 185
Advisory Committee for Trade Policy and Negotiations (ACTPN), 34
Affair, The (Snow), 39, 193
affirmative action, 62, 127, 142
Afrocentrists, -ism, 145, 184
Ageless Bodies, Timeless Minds (Chopra), 29, 191
Aikath-Gyaltsen, Indrani, 32
Albert, Peter, 83
American Association for the Advancement of Science, 26
American Historical Association (AHA), 117-118
American Historical Review, 117
American Scholar, 23, 50, 190
Amistad (film), 27
And the Walls Came Tumbling Down (Abernathy), 185
Angelou, Maya, 29, 191
animal sacrifices, 139
Aristotle, 29, 145
Arizona, 100-103
Arizona State University, 15, 52, 87, 138
Arminians, -ism, 158, 162
Atlanta, 85, 92, 94, 97-99, 107, 124-125, 127, 175, 177-178
Atlanta Independent, 126
Atlanta Journal/Constitution, 93, 98, 109, 177
Autobiography of Malcolm X, The, 143-144

Babalu, 24
Babbitt, Bruce, 176
Babington, Charles, 14, 46-47, 93, 109, 194
Bach, Johann Sebastian, 29
Ballantine Books, 32
Balthasar, Hans Urs von, 4, 155
Balz, Dan, 97
Barry, Marion, 141
Barth, Karl, 3-4, 151, 154-156
Baseline Essays, 145
Bate, Walter Jackson, 51
Bateman, Merrill J., 40
BBC, 111
Bearing the Cross: Martin Luther King, Jr., and the Southern Christian Leadership Crisis (Garrow), 58, 87, 106, 197
Bennett, William, 35-37, 40, 184
Berlin, Kenneth, 35
Bernstein, Richard, 21, 62, 189, 198
Bettelheim, Bruno, 29, 191
Biden, Joseph, 26
Biographia Literaria (Coleridge), 50-51
Biographical Dictionary of Early Pennsylvania Legislators, 38
Black English, 142
Boggs, Wade, 141
Bond, Julian, 178, 181
Book of Virtues, The (Bennett), 36-37
Boozer, Jack, 13, 23, 66, 90, 94, 102, 114, 183, 195
Bosley, Harold, 133

Boston Globe, 39-40, 193
Boston University, 2-4, 11-13, 16, 23, 38-39, 45, 47, 51, 54, 66-69, 82, 85-86, 88, 90-91, 94-96, 105, 107-109, 111, 113, 115-116, 124-126, 132, 137-138, 141, 150, 153-154, 184, 196
Bowers, Neal, 44, 195
Bradford, Zee, 180
Branch, Taylor, 181-182
Brandeis University, 174
Brawley, Tawana, 144
Brecht, Bertolt, 139
Brigham Young University (BYU), 40, 193
Brightman, Edgar Sheffield, 3, 153-154
British Petroleum, 180
Brown, Dee, 28
Brown v. Board of Education, 164
Buchanan, Patrick, 39, 193
Burke, Edmund, 106
Bury My Heart at Wounded Knee (Brown), 28
Butterfield, Fox, 39, 193

Calvin, John, 3, 156-158, 162
Carey, Archibald, 45, 133, 140, 183
Carlson, Allan, 19
Carson, Clayborne, 2, 5, 22, 47, 51-53, 56, 67, 69, 86, 89-90, 92-94, 96-99, 105-106, 109-112, 123-124, 129, 131-132, 137-138, 197

Cartwright, John, 138
Cassler, Robert, 140
Cato Institute, 35, 192
CBS, 179
Center for Democratic Renewal, 146
Certain Trumpets: The Call of Leaders (Wills), 45, 195
Chase-Riboud, Barbara, 27
Cheney, Lynne, 47, 96
Chesterfield, Lord, 23
Chicago Sun-Times, 27
Chicago Tribune, 46, 69, 108-109, 191, 193
China, 41-42
Chinese Scientific News, 41
Chopra, Deepak, 29, 191
Christian Coalition, 146
Christian ethics, 167, 170
Chronicle of Higher Education, The, 37, 55-56, 60, 69, 82, 106, 139-140, 193-195, 197
Chronicles: A Magazine of American Culture, 19, 46, 82, 95-96, 174, 189
Church Dogmatics (Barth), 3, 156
civil rights movement, 9, 12, 23, 45, 47, 57-58, 62, 83, 132, 134, 143, 164, 174, 177
Civil Rights: Rhetoric or Reality? (Sowell), 21, 189
Clark, Dick, 179
Classical Rhetoric and Its Christian and Secular Traditions from Ancient to Modern Times (Kennedy), 48, 195

Cleopatra, 145
Clinton, Bill, 34, 46, 146
Clinton, Chelsea, 142
Cobb, Joe, 34-35, 192
Coca-Cola, 180
Cohen, Jeff, 183
Coleridge, Samuel Taylor, 12, 47, 49-52
Columbia Journalism Review, 26, 190
Columbia University, 143, 185
Commentary, 36
Concert, The (Kadare), 29
Conjuring Culture: Biblical Formations of Black America (Smith), 166
Cook, Louise, 183
Cooper-Lewter, Nicholas, 163
Cornell University, 42
Countering the Conspiracy to Destroy Black Boys, 144
Cousteau: A Biography (Violet), 22
Cousteau, Jacques, 22
Cranes' Morning (Gyaltsen), 32
Cribb, John, 36
critical race theory, 142
Crozer Theological Seminary, 88, 124-126, 128-130
cultural relativism, 24, 55
Culture War, 6, 21-22, 25, 139, 149, 189
Cumont, Franz, 129

Dabney, Robert L., 157-158, 160

Dailey, Janet, 33-34
Daily Report (Fulton County, Georgia), 181
Dallas Morning News, 100, 184
Dante, 31, 192
Darsee, John, 41
Davis, George Washington, 129-131
de Man, Paul, 111-112
De Quincey, Thomas, 49
deconstructionism, 24, 111
Democrats, 34-35
Denver Post, 27
DePalma, Anthony, 99
DeWolf, Harold L., 3-4, 81, 90-91, 113-114, 154, 156
Dictionary of American Negro Biography, 145
Disuniting of America, The (Schlesinger), 145, 189
diversity, 21-22, 24, 33, 55, 63, 135, 175
Dogmatics in Outline (Barth), 155
Drew, Charles, 145
Duke University, 181

Early Theological Writings (Hegel), 156
Ebenezer Baptist Church, 124
Ebonics, 142
Echo of Lions (Chase-Riboud), 27
Emory University, 66, 69-71, 93, 97
Engell, James, 51
Enslin, Morton, 125

environmentalism, 133
Epistle to the Romans, The (Barth), 155
Epstein, Jacob, 28
Eros and Modernization (Sokolow), 38
Esquire, 26

Feder, Ned, 41, 46
female circumcision, 139
feminism, 133
Ferrier, J.C., 51
Finley, Karen, 24
First Things, 40
Fischer, David Hackett, 174
Fleming, Thomas, 19, 67-68, 96
Follett, Ken, 28
Ford Motor Company, 180
Forgers and Critics: Creativity and Duplicity in Western Scholarship (Grafton), 62, 198
Fosdick, Harry Emerson, 88
Fraud and Fallible Judgment: Varieties of Deception in the Social and Behavioral Sciences (Pallone and Hennessy), 42, 194
Frazier, Shervert, 41
Frye, Northrop, 29

Gandhi, Mahatma, 119, 150, 167
Gardner, William E., 126
Garrow, David, 58, 87, 106, 180-182, 197

gay rights, 61, 133
Genovese, Eugene, 6, 52-53, 56, 99, 149, 196
gerrymandering, 142
Gershwin, George, 27
Gettysburg Address, 107
Gigot, Paul, 34, 192
Girardeau, John, 157
Gogh, Vincent van, 30
Goldsmith, Oliver, 49
Goudge, Elizabeth, 32
Grafton, Anthony, 62, 198
Gramsci, Antonio, 24
Grapes of Wrath, The, 26

Haley, Alex, 28, 143-144
Halliday, W.R., 129
Hamilton, J. Wallace, 133
Harnack, Adolph von, 158
Harrison, Eric, 177
Harvard Medical School, 41
Harwood, Richard, 98
Hegel, Georg Wilhelm Friedrich, 70, 81, 150, 153, 156
Hellman, Lillian, 137
Hennessy, James J., 42, 194
Heritage Foundation, 34
hero, hero-worship, 17, 21-23, 50, 107, 119, 140, 177, 184
Himmelfarb, Gertrude, 36, 40
Hirayama, Takeshi, 42
Hodge, Charles, 162

Hoffman, Ronald, 83
Hollywood, 38-39, 144
Holst, Gustav, 27
Homer, 29
homosexuals, -phobia, 15, 60-61, 94
Hoover, J. Edgar, 83
Horace, 49
Hughes, Gary Owens, 38
Human Events, 145
human rights, 55, 61
Humphrey, Hubert, 26
Hunter, James Davison, 21, 189

I Shared the Dream: The Pride, Passion and Politics of the First Black Woman Senator From Kentucky (Powers), 59, 197
IBM, 180
Iliad (Homer), 29
Inman, Bobby Ray, 26
Institute on Religion and Democracy, 146
Institutes of the Christian Religion (Calvin), 157
Institutio oratoria (Quintilian), 57, 196
Intellectual Properties Management (IPM), 179-183
International Monetary Fund, 34
Ivans, Molly, 29

Jackson, Jesse, 143, 178, 183

Jefferson, Thomas, 133, 173
Jeremiah, 128, 159
Jesus Christ, 131, 152, 159, 165, 168-169
Johnson, Frank, 65, 94
Johnson, Samuel, 30, 58, 70, 134, 139, 191, 197
Jones, Phillip, 179
Journal of American History, 51, 69, 92-93, 96-97, 112

Kadare, Ismael, 29
Kaiser, Robert, 98
Kamen, Al, 36, 192
Kennedy, George, 48, 195
Kennedy, John, 26, 45, 109, 184-185
Kennedy, Robert, 26
Kenyon, Kenneth, 41
Key to Rebecca, The (Follett), 28
Kimball, Roger, 21, 134, 189
Kincaid, James, 29, 31, 38
King, Coretta, 111, 177, 183
King, Dexter, 175-176, 179-180, 182
King, Don, 144
King estate, 175, 179-183
King family, 5, 126, 175-183
King, Martin Luther, Jr., *Early Life*: 88-89, 124-127; *Assassination*: 175; *Moral failings*: 59, 65, 87, 101-102, 185; *Holiday and Controversy*: 100-103; *Dissertation* ("A Comparison of the Conceptions of God in the

Thinking of Paul Tillich and Henry Nelson Wieman): 2-4, 12-14, 22-23, 45-46, 51-54, 65-105, 108, 111, 115-116, 123-126, 132, 137-138, 151-164, 195; *Nobel Peace Prize and Speech:* 87, 133; *Other Writings, Speeches, and Sermons: Strength to Love,* 88; *Stride Toward Freedom,* 88; "Letter From Birmingham Jail," 88; "A Study of Mithraism," 129; "Contemporary Continental Theology," 163; "I Have a Dream," 45, 133, 140, 165; "Karl Barth's Conception of God," 154-155; "Ritual," 127-128; "The Humanity and Divinity of Jesus," 131; "The Origin of Religion in the Race," 130-131; "Pilgrimage to Nonviolence," 133; "The Significant Contributions of Jeremiah to Religious Thought," 128-129; "The Sources of Fundamentalism," 130; "The Influence of the Mystery Religions on Christianity," 131; "Religion's Answer to the Problem of Evil," 131; *Legacy:* 9, 11-12, 15, 83, 101-102, 133, 149-150, 170-171, 175-176, 178, 183-186; *Nonviolence:* 9, 133, 164-170

King, Martin Luther, Sr., 124-125

King Papers Project, 22, 47, 51-52, 67, 69, 82, 88, 91-92, 97, 109-110, 112, 123, 159, 183

King v. Mister Maestro, Inc., 140

Kinnock, Neil, 26

Kinsley, Michael, 27-28

Knowledge of God and the Service of God, The (Barth), 155

LaFollette, Marcel C., 43, 194

Lang, Jeffrey M., 35

Lasch, Christopher, 21, 135, 189

Last Brother, The (McGinniss), 28

Last Crusade, The (McKnight), 83

Le monde du silence (film), 22

Le petit prince de Belleville (Beyala), 44

Le Point, 44, 194

Leavitt, David, 29, 60-61, 197-198

Lefkowitz, Mary, 21, 190

Leo, John, 139

Les honneurs perdus (Beyala), 43

Levison, Stanley, 59, 133

Liberators, The (film), 144

Liberty Lobby, 95

Lieberman, Trudy, 26, 190

Lincoln, Abraham, 29, 106

Lincoln University, 166

Lire, 44

Lischer, Richard, 58, 181, 197

Logan, Rayford, 145

Los Angeles Times, 27

Lowery, Joseph E., 182

Luker, Ralph, 66, 70, 86, 94, 110

Mailer, Norman, 28
Maitre, H. Joachim, 38-40, 112
Malcom X, 143-144, 177, 185-186
Mallon, Thomas, 23, 31, 49, 51, 54, 116, 190, 192, 196
Mandela, Nelson, 177
Mapplethorpe, Robert, 24
Marable, Manning, 185-186
Marshall, Thurgood, 164, 166
Martial, 31
Martin Luther King Jr. Center for Non-violent Social Change (King Center), 107, 175-176, 178, 180, 183
Martin Luther King, Jr., Plagiarism Story, The (Pappas), 1, 150, 189
Martin Luther King, Jr., Professor of Social Ethics, 138, 184
Martin Luther King Jr. Time Machine and Interactive Museum, 176
Marx, Karl, 119, 165
Marxism, -ist, 55, 165
Massie, Robert, 26
Maxwell, Megan, 86
McCabe, Donald, 26
McCarthy, Mary, 137
McFarland, Thomas, 51
McGinniss, Joe, 28
McKnight, Gerald, 83
McLean, George, 110
Media Beat, 183
Medved, Michael, 39
Meres, Francis, 48
Meyer, Leonard, 29, 191

Miles, William, 144
Miller, Keith, 15, 52, 54-61, 87-88, 119-120, 123, 132-135, 138-142, 196-198
minority rights, 135
Mitchell, Henry H., 163-164
Monroe, Marilyn, 28
Monty Python, 28
Morehouse College, 124, 127, 159, 175
Muelder, Walter, 105, 107
multiculturalism, 6, 21-22, 24-25, 55, 62, 189
Murchison, William, 100, 184
Music, the Arts, and Ideas (Meyer), 29, 191
Mysteries of Mithra, The (Cumont), 129

Nation, The, 26, 190
National Association of Evangelicals, 146
National Basketball Association (NBA), 101-102
National Church Arson Task Force, 146
National Council of Churches, 146
National Endowment for the Arts (NEA), 35
National Endowment for the Humanities (NEH), 35, 47, 82, 90, 96, 116, 183, 195
National Football League (NFL), 101, 103

National Front (France), 44
National Institutes of Health (NIH), 41, 43
National League of Cities, 101-102
National Park Service, 176-177
National Science Foundation, 43
Nature, 42, 194
Naughton, John, 28
Nazis, Nazism, 14-15
neo-orthodoxy, 159
neoconservatives, 174
Neusner, Jacob, 1, 17
New Republic, 14, 46, 52, 93, 99, 109, 195-196
New York Observer, 28, 190
New York Times, 26-27, 32, 60, 93, 99, 106, 109, 138, 175, 178-179, 181-183, 190, 193, 195
New York Times Book Review, 46, 99, 195, 198
New York Times Magazine, 41, 60, 194, 198
New Yorker, The, 29, 36-37, 191
News Weekly (Australian), 139
Niebuhr, Reinhold, 119, 163
Nietzsche, Friedrich, 137
Nightline, 26
Nissenbaum, Stephen, 37-38, 82, 193
Nobile, Philip, 143-144, 191
Noonan, Peggy, 110
North American Free Trade Agreement (NAFTA), 35, 192
Northwestern University, 44

Norton, Eleanor Holmes, 184

Oates, Stephen, 29
Observer (London), 28
Odyssey (Homer), 29
Orlando Sentinel, 27
Ovid, 48
Oxford University, 38

Pagan Background of Early Christianity, The (Halliday), 129
Pallone, Nathaniel J., 42, 194
Papers of Martin Luther King, Jr., The (*see also* "King Papers Project"), 2, 123
Pappas, Theodore, 1-2, 5, 9, 11-13, 15-16, 96, 102, 150
Parade, 59, 197
Pasadena City College, 139
Passages (Sheehy), 28
PBS, 144
Peking University, 42
Pelikan, Jaroslav, 169
Peretz, Martin, 14, 99
Phantom of the Opera, The (film), 30
Phenomenology of Mind (Hegel), 153
Philadelphia Inquirer, 38, 192
Philosophy of Hegel, The (Stace), 153
Pilate, Pontius, 168
Plato, 29, 113, 150
Playboy, 143

Plot It Yourself (Stout), 43, 194
Plotinus, 70, 81
pluralism, 22, 55, 135
Poe, Edgar Allan, 44
political correctness, 9, 14, 22, 24, 62
Pollitt, Katha, 28
polygamy, 139
Pope, Alexander, 49
Powers, Georgia Davis, 59, 197
Preacher King, The (Lischer), 58, 181, 197
Princeton Theological Seminary, 156
Profiles in Courage (Kennedy), 45
Promise Keepers, 146
Publishers Weekly, 32, 143, 191
Pythagoras, 48, 145

Quintilian, 57, 197

race-norming, 142
race relations, racism, -ists, 2-3, 5, 10, 12, 14-16, 62, 143-144, 146, 164-165, 171, 174, 176, 178, 183-184, 186
"rage defense," the, 63
Randall, John Herman, 115
Raspberry, William, 106
Ray, James Earl, 175
Reader's Digest, 39
Reed, John Shelton, 47, 95-96, 107, 195

Renaissance, 48, 196
Republicans (GOP), 34-35, 184
reverse (inverse) discrimination, 142-143, 184
Richard, Michel, 44
Ringle, Ken, 176-178, 180
Ritschl, Albrecht Benjamin, 159
Roberts, Nora, 33
Rockford Institute, The, 1, 19, 95, 189
Rogers, Cornish, 91
Roots (Haley), 28, 143-144, 191
Roots of Alex Haley, The (film), 144
Rosemary Tree, The (Goudge), 32
Rosenblum, Nina, 144
Rules, The, 28
Russell, Penny, 91
Rutgers University, 113

Sack, Kevin, 175, 179-180, 182
Safire, William, 26
San Francisco Chronicle, 27
Schilling, S. Paul, 4-5, 53-54, 91, 107
Schleiermacher, Friedrich Daniel Ernst, 159
Schlesinger, Arthur, Jr., 21, 145, 189
Schwartzkopff, Frances, 98
Science, 41, 194
Scott, Walter, 59, 197
Seneca the Elder, 48, 195
Serrano, Andres, 24
Sex, Diet, and Debility in Jacksonian America (Nissenbaum), 37

Shakespeare, William, 48, 50, 135, 198
Shalit, Ruth, 29
Sharpton, Al, 144
Shaw, Peter, 23, 50-51, 190, 194
Sheehy, Gail, 28
Sidney, Sir P., 49
Silber, John, 68, 138, 141
Simon & Schuster, 36
Sinkler, Rebecca, 99
Slate, 27-28
slavery, 142, 161, 165
Sleeper, Jim, 27
Smith, Theophus H., 166
Snow, C.P., 39, 193
Socrates, 29
Sokolow, Jayme, 37-38, 116-117
Solomon, Norman, 183
Sontag, Susan, 24
Sorensen, Theodore, 45, 110
Southern Christian Leadership Conference (SCLC), 182
Southern Front: History and Politics in the Culture War (Genovese), 149
Soviets, 186
Sowell, Thomas, 21, 145, 189
Speaking Truth to Power: Essays on Race, Resistance, and Radicalism (Marable), 185
Spender, Sir Stephen, 60-61, 198
Spielberg, Steven, 27
Spotlight, The, 95

St. Louis-Dispatch, 27
St. Paul, 140
Stace, W.T., 153
Stanford Observer, 105
Stanford University, 22, 30, 67, 69, 86, 184
Stealing into Print: Fraud, Plagiarism, and Misconduct in Scientific Publishing (LaFollette), 43, 194
Stewart, Walter, 40, 46
Stolen Words: Forays into the Origins and Ravages of Plagiarism (Mallon), 23, 31, 49-51, 116, 190, 192, 196
Stone, Oliver, 179
Stout, Rex, 43, 194
Stove, R.J., 139
Stowe, Jay, 28, 190
Streitfeld, David, 33, 191-192, 197
Sunday Telegraph, The (London), 65, 67, 69, 94, 105, 110
Sunstone, 40
Swaggart, Jimmy, 56
Sykes, Charles, 21
Systematic Theology (Tillich), 79, 81, 115, 162

Tagliabue, Paul, 101, 103
Tchaikovsky, Petr Ilich, 27
Temple University, 38
Tennyson, Alfred, 49
Teresa, Mother, 28

Texas Tech University, 116
Theology of Karl Barth, The (Balthasar), 4, 155
Theology of Paul Tillich, The (Randall), 115
Thoreau, Henry David, 167
Thornwell, James Henley, 158, 160
Tillich, Paul, 3-4, 68-71, 73, 78-81, 97, 102, 114-115, 153-154, 159, 183
Time, 27, 191
Time-Warner, 179, 182-183
tolerance, 13, 22, 33, 175
Tolstoy, Leo, 167-168
Tooley, Mark, 146
Trinity College, 38
Tseng, Scheffer C.G., 41
Tucker, Cynthia, 177

University of Alabama, Birmingham, 42
University of California, Los Angeles, 113
University of Hong Kong, 42
University of Illinois, 60
University of Nebraska Press, 111-112
University of North Carolina at Chapel Hill, 47
University of Oregon, 30
USA Today, 179

Uses of Enchantment: The Meaning and Importance of Fairy Tales (Bettelheim), 29

Valide (Chase-Riboud), 27
Vanity Fair, 28, 190
Vietnam, 133
Village Voice, 143, 191
Violet, Bernard, 22, 190
voice merging, 54, 57, 60-61, 63, 88, 132, 134, 139, 183
Voices of Deliverance: The Language of Martin Luther King, Jr., and Its Sources (Miller), 52, 123, 196-197

Wagner, Richard, 27
Waldheim, Kurt, 111
Waldman, Peter, 85, 98
Wall Street Journal, 34, 39, 69, 85, 93-94, 96, 98-99, 109-110, 123, 177, 192
Wallace, Mike, 179
Ward, Robert, 144
Washington Post, 27, 33, 36, 69, 93, 97, 109, 176-177, 180, 190-193, 197
We Shall Overcome: Martin Luther King, Jr., and the Black Freedom Struggle (Albert and Hoffman), 83
Wellesley College, 184
Westling, Jon, 13, 68-69, 82, 95-96, 105, 107-109, 137, 141

Westminster College (England), 38
While England Sleeps (Leavitt), 29, 60
Wieman, Henry Nelson, 4, 68-69, 160
Wieseltier, Leon, 99
Wild Oats (Epstein), 28
Wills, Garry, 44-46, 194
Wilson, Flip, 33
Wilson, Kenneth, 38
witchcraft, witches, 24, 139
Wofford, Harris, 88, 133
Wolfe, Nero, 43
Wood, Peter, 137-138, 141
Word of God and the Word of Man, The
    (Barth), 155
Words for the Taking: The Hunt for a Pla-
    giarist (Bowers), 44, 195
World Bank, 34
World Trade Organization, 34

Young, Andrew, 133
Youngblood, Mtamanika, 177

Zhangliang, Chen, 41

Quotable Quotes From

THE DISADVANTAGES OF BEING EDUCATED
and other essays

by
Albert J. Nock

"Man tends always to satisfy his needs and desires with the least possible exertion."
— *The Gods' Lookout*, 1934

"Perhaps one reason for the falling-off of belief in a continuance of conscious existence is to be found in the quality of life that most of us lead."
— *Earning Immortality*, 1930

"In speaking of instruction as equivalent to education, or vice versa, we misuse language."
— *Toward A New Quality Product*, 1926

"When the Declaration of Independence was drafted Mr. Jefferson wrote, 'life, liberty and the pursuit of happiness' . . . his colleagues . . . let the alteration stand . . . It was a revolutionary change."
— *Life, Liberty, And . . .*, 1935

"Civilization is the progressive humanization of men in society . . ."
— *Toadstools*, 1923

"In addition to our present system of schools, colleges and universities which are doing first-class work as training schools, we ought to have a few educational institutions."
— *The Disadvantages of Being Educated*, 1942

Albert J. Nock (1870-1945) was a
radical, in the venerable sense of the
word: one whose ideas cut to the root
and make you think again about things
previously taken for granted.

ISBN 0-87319-041-6
224 pages, Trade Paper, $14.95

The Disadvantages of Being Educated and other essays

and other books by Albert J. Nock are available
through your local bookstore or from the publisher,

HALLBERG PUBLISHING CORPORATION

P.O. Box 23985, Tampa, FL 33623
Phone 800-633-7627 • Fax 800-253-7323